CLIMBERS' CLUB GUIDES TO WALES

1 Carneddau
2 The Glyders and Tryfan
3 Llanberis
4 Clogwyn Du'r Arddu
5 Lliwedd
6 Snowdon South
7 Anglesey
8 Cwm Silyn & Cwellyn

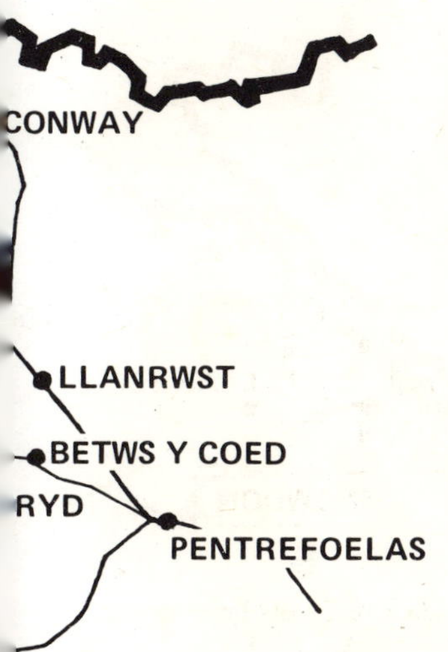

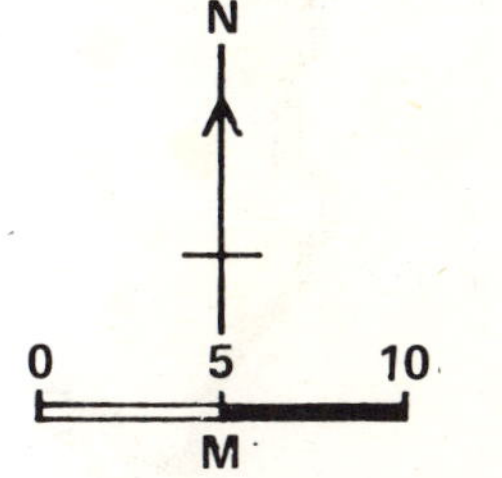

Revised Guide Book Areas 1976

First Edition 1963
by H I Banner and P Crew

Second Edition 1967
by H I Banner and P Crew

Third Edition 1976
by A Sharp

IBSN 0. 901601 30 6

front cover	The East Buttress. Photo: Ken Wilson
back cover	Alec Sharp on Jelly Roll. Photo: Ken Wilson

Printed by Allied Publicity Services (Manchester) Limited

CLIMBERS' CLUB GUIDES TO WALES
Edited by Robert Moulton

4

Clogwyn du'r Arddu

by Alec Sharp

Diagrams by R B Evans and map by Ken Wilson

Cover photographs by Ken Wilson

Published by the CLIMBERS' CLUB
with financial assistance from the
BRITISH MOUNTAINEERING COUNCIL

CONTENTS

ACKNOWLEDGEMENTS

I would like to thank everyone who has helped with this guide, especially Geoff Milburn for all the information concerning the Far West, and the previous guidebook writers for the basis of this guide. I would also like to thank Brian Evans for his excellent sketches, Janet Wyatt for typing out the manuscript for the guide, and Ken Wilson for the cover photographs and cover design.

Finally thanks to Chris Dale, Steve Humphries, Dave Midlane and John Zangwill for many happy days spent on Cloggy.

A S 1976

Introduction

The cliffs face north and are only visited by the sun in early morning and late evening, so that they dry slowly after prolonged rain. Their sombre appearance, sweeping lines and steep angle produce an impressive atmosphere, which gives the climbs great character and often makes the leads more difficult than might be expected. This is especially true in imperfect conditions.

The climbs, with only one or two exceptions such as White Slab and Llithrig, are described in the most free style in which they have been climbed. One or two changes have been made in the gradings, both numerical and adjectival. The numerical grades refer to the difficulty of top-roping the climb and so the strenousness of the climb is an important factor on the steeper routes. The adjectival grading system has been given a three tier Extreme grade, with Hard Extreme reserved for routes of great seriousness or very great difficulty, or both. Where aid of any form is used the number of points of aid is given in brackets after the adjectival grade. Some of the very well protected climbs have been downgraded since it is felt that the adjectival grade should be biased towards the factors other than technical difficulty and strenuousness to avoid duplication of the numerical system. For these reasons it may be found that the slab routes are easier propositions for their grades, than the steeper walls, because the greater seriousness of the slab routes often result in a higher adjectival grade than a wall with an equivalent numerical grade.

As usual with the passing of time, illicit pegs find their way on to routes originally done without. It is to be hoped that pitons not described in the text will be removed by parties finding them.

The now common star system for quality has been introduced. Cloggy is such a fine cliff that I have had to cut down the number of stars given with the result that many routes here are better than routes with an equal number of stars in other areas.

In all the route descriptions, "right" and "left" are given assuming the climber to be facing the cliff.

Historical

The first recorded rock climb in Britain took place on Cloggy in 1798 when the Rev. Peter Williams and Rev. W. Bingley climbed the Eastern Terrace, but this was an isolated event for the cliff and it was not until 1905 that climbers really attempted to climb the cliff by a more important line. This was when the Abraham brothers visited the cliff and tried the deep chimneys on the East Buttress that are today taken by Chimney Route. However they did not get very far, but they climbed the East Wall Climb. A trivial route but important as the first proper climb, and one made by outsiders from the establishment.

In 1927 the first major route was climbed after several attempts. The climb was Pigott's Climb, put up by Fred Pigott, Lindley Henshaw, Morley Wood and John Burton, a route which proved to be harder than many subsequent climbs on the cliff. In 1928 Jack Longland, with Pigott, Smythe, Eversden and Morley Wood, climbed the thin slab bounding the West Buttress on the left. It must have been a very serious route at the time with very sparse protection. In fact the first fatality on Cloggy was on Longland's some thirty years later. Although these routes did not represent an advance in technique, being no harder than some other existing climbs, they marked a psychological breakthrough because each climb took the only line up a truly impressive piece of rock. 1930 to 1933 saw a fine series of major routes on Cloggy, mainly the work of Colin Kirkus, but Maurice Linnell, a superb technician, Alf Bridge, A.B. Hargreaves, Ted Hicks, Ivan Waller, Graham Macphee, Menlove Edwards, and Pigott and Wood all played their part. Kirkus put up a fine series of routes with Great Slab, Chimney Route, Pedestal Crack, Terrace Crack, Curving Crack, Birthday Crack and the Direct Finish to the East Buttress, not to be equalled for many years. At this time Linnell put in two impressive performances with his Narrow Slab, the hardest route on the cliff at that time, and with his on sight solo first ascent of the first pitch of Curving Crack.

Nothing much happened for a few years except for Jubilee Climb and Cox's ascent of Sunset Crack, although it was in this period that Arthur Birtwistle climbed the Drainpipe Crack, a remarkable performance, but failed on the continuation crack now taken by November. In 1941, after several attempts, Menlove Edwards climbed Bow-Shaped Slab and four years later Campbell and Cox found Sheaf, while attempting White Slab.

The period after the war saw a better equipped climber, with Ex W.D. equipment readily available, but it was still a few years before nylon ropes became popular. The main figures of this period are Peter Harding, John Lawton and Arnold Carsten. Harding, like Kirkus and Lawton climbed all the routes on the cliff and added a girdle to the West Buttress. He also climbed and reversed the crux of Pinnacle Flake, an impressive performance, as many a modern leader would agree. Harding's new outlook on the use of pegs enabled him to raise the standard of climbing above the pre-war level and to lay a foundation for the future.

The next climber to make a mark on the cliff was Joe Brown. Having no links with the climbing establishment Brown and his friends just took climbs as they found them, with no preconceptions or traditions to hold them back. In three days in the summer of 1949 Brown and Sorrell climbed all thirteen of the major routes on Cloggy to gain a familiarity with the cliff equalled only by the most experienced climbers of the day, which they had won by years of effort. Brown then tried Vember in appalling conditions but he fell from the second pitch, cutting two strands of his hemp rope.

His first new route on the cliff was Diglyph, where the second had to have a knotted rope beside him to pull on if necessary. Also that year Brown climbed Vember with Whillans, who was only seventeen at the time. Two weeks later he added The Boulder, a climb remarkable for the fact that his second, Moseley, declined to follow and so another rope had to be tied on to Brown's climbing rope and Brown continued, fixing runners by knotting loops in the rope. 1952 saw Brown's most active year, with six routes in about as many weeks, three of them with Don Whillans, with whom he shared leads. This decade was dominated by Brown and Whillans, with Streetly's ascent of Bloody Slab being the only important new route made by an outsider to the Rock and Ice until 1959. Of the rest of the Rock and Ice only Moseley made an important contribution when he sneaked in and climbed White Slab the day before Whillans did it. While Brown climbed the largest number of new routes on the cliff, Whillans put up three of the most impressive. Taurus, Woubits and Slanting Slab were all extremely serious routes, with the former two being strenuous and loose besides. All three achieved tremendous reputations.

1957 saw Brown climbing The Mostest and then climbing November with about eight chockstones for aid.

1959 was a superb year. The sun shone and many of the hard routes were repeated by climbers from outside the Rock and Ice. The most prominent of these was Hugh Banner who in that year added two major routes to the cliff, Ghecko Groove and Troach. Troach was an important route for it showed the possibility of climbing the big unprotected walls. At this time also, Brown had climbed most of what is now the first pitch of Great Wall. It took the new group of young climbers the whole of the next year to find its feet, during which time various people worked on the problem of girdling the Pinnacle. The most significant contribution to this was Banner's ascent of The Hand Traverse. The next year marked the coming of age of the new generation and the start of one of the finest series of routes put up on the cliff. Troach had opened the way for the walls to be climbed, and Soper and Crew put up Scorpio on the neighbouring wall on the right. At the end of August these two also solved the problem of the Pinnacle Girdle in three days. After this Crew teamed up with Ingle to establish a partnership rivalling that of Brown and Whillans, and one which was responsible for some of the best routes on the cliff, routes such as Serth, The Shadow, Haemagoblin, West Buttress Eliminate, and culminating in what must have been one of the most serious and hard routes of the time, Great Wall. The winter of 1962/63 was harsh and The Black Cleft was climbed as an ice climb by Ingle and Boysen, and it was later repeated by Rowland Edwards and by Brown. The following year Crew added another fine route, The Boldest, which at the time had the reputation of being one of the hardest routes in Britain and was the first route on Cloggy to have an expansion bolt.

In 1965 Brown came back with three new routes on the Far East, but the most significant event was the emergence of Rowland Edwards with his ascent of Diwedd Groove, which was not to be repeated for ten years. Edwards was obsessed with the many unclimbed slabs on the West and the next year produced Spartacus, Mynedd, Fibrin and the New Girdle of the West, this last being the second route to use expansion bolts. Unfortunately Mynedd, Spartacus and the original line of Diwedd Groove all have such unpleasant starts that they will probably never become popular.

During the late sixties it became popular to eliminate aid from the existing routes and it was in this period that climbs such as Pinnacle Arête and Shrike were first climbed free, although it was not until the next decade that the routes with major aid sections were free climbed. The first one of these was November which was climbed by Richard McHardy in 1970, who also made an on sight solo of the top pitch of Woubits. Another notable solo around this time was Alan Rouse's solo of The Boldest, which he had previously led on his first visit to the cliff. The demise of The Boldest was completed when the bolt was chopped in 1973. Rouse then put up a route of his own, Gemini, to the left of The Boldest and this in turn acquired a reputation as one of the hardest and most serious climbs on the cliff until Ray Evans made the second ascent, without either of the two protection pegs.

Besides making the first free ascent of Daurigol with Pasquill and Syrett, Ray Evans began to climb the first thirty feet of most of the then unclimbed lines; this paid off when he managed to complete the Stomach Traverse, Jelly Roll and Curving Arête, with Chris Rogers, and partnered Hank Pasquill on The Leech. Curving Arête was a particularly noteworthy performance, being achieved without aid or pegs, despite Crew's earlier comment: 'Can't be done. Only two jugs. It would need at least four pegs.', and it is one of the most serious pitches on the cliff. In that year, 1971, Boysen climbed a new direct route up Great Slab, which he called Syth.

The next two years were quiet and 1974 did not bring much except for Phil Bartlett's route Quiver, up the left arête of Bow-Shaped Slab, and the second ascent of Curving Arête, but 1975 saw an explosion of activity with a host of new routes and several important free ascents.

Th main contributor to the new routes was Rowland Edwards with The Sweeper, Silhouette and Medi. Medi is a particularly impressive climb, very hard and with the thought of a fall into Curving Crack always in the back of the mind. All were cleaned out by abseil and then climbed free. Cliff Phillips came out of hibernation and worked out the section of cliff around the Steep Band to give some hard climbs while Alec Sharp cleaned up the left hand groove above Great Wall and climbed it free to produce a very difficult climb, Blancmange Sandwich. Arniş Strapcans added a fine route to the Pinnacle with The Spire and also climbed two more routes on the Far East.

The major free ascent of 1975 was John Allen's ascent of Great Wall. First climbed with about eight points of aid, this was gradually whittled down to one point but Allen dispensed with this to make Great Wall into probably the hardest climb on the cliff. Woubits Left Hand was also climbed free by Alec Sharp, and Capricorn had its second ascent from Sharp and Chris Dale, who managed to free the crux pitch, which had used three pegs on the first ascent.

More information about the period up to 1966 can be found in 'The Black Cliff' by Crew, Soper and Wilson (Kaye and Ward, 1971).

Approaches

Snowdon throws down from Carnedd Ugain a north ridge towards Llanberis and a west ridge to Snowdon Ranger. Clogwyn Du'r Arddu (probably meaning the black cliff of the black height) lies on the north face of the west ridge and looks out over Cwm Brwynog, the cwm between these ridges, towards the north ridge which carries the railway. At the foot of the cliff is Llyn Du'r Arddu at a height of 1901 feet; the top of the cliff is about 2,500 feet.

The cliff can easily be reached from most parts of central Snowdonia. For those with their own means of transport, the best way is to drive to Llanberis and up the narrow road opposite the Royal Victoria Hotel. Follow this up the steep hill, through several gates (please close them after you), for about a mile and a half to Hafoty Newydd, a farm on the slopes below Cwm Brwynog. Climbers are requested not to park in the passing bays on this road; instead cars should be left at the start of the Lanberis path or in accordance with any future arrangements that may be introduced during the life of this book. From Hafoty Newydd walk up the railway and the track until well past Half-Way House, and, where the main track steepens, keep right along the miners' track which leads to the old copper mines and continues as a small path contouring round to the cliff. The best approach by foot from the Llanberis Pass is up Cwm Glas Mawr to Clogwyn Station and down to the track above Half-Way House; and from the south side by the Snowdon Ranger path which crosses the top of the cliff. An hour and a half is ample for any of these ways, depending on how long one spends recovering in Half-Way House.

The Far Far East Buttress

This is the small compact buttress higher than and to the left of everything else. A curving green slab runs into enormous overhangs and provides the first route. To the right of this are steep broken walls. It is possible to descend the loose gully to the left of the buttress.

Boomerang 180 feet Hard Very Severe (1959)
A pleasant first pitch but a loose top pitch. Scramble to the foot of the green slab.
1 90 feet. Climb the crack in the centre of the slab to the groove on the right. Climb this and move left at the overhangs to a ledge. The left edge of the slab can be climbed all the way.
2 90 feet. Move up right past a grass ledge beneath the large overhang, and climb past a pinnacle to the arête. Move around the arête and into a niche. Swing right and then back left again to ledges. Continue up slightly right, finishing with a traverse across a steep wall.

Variation
2a 90 feet. Climb the rib on the left of the overhang and traverse across the lip of the overhang to join the normal route at a similar standard.

Soledad Brother 150 feet Hard Very Severe (1971)
Climbs a steep corner groove fifty feet right of Boomerang. Traverse up to the right from the foot of Boomerang's slab.
Start: Below and to the left of the corner groove below a left slanting ten foot crack.
1 50 feet. Climb the crack and after a few feet of broken ground traverse right to below a steep right-angled corner. Climb the corner to a small stance and peg belay.
2 100 feet. Climb the right hand side of the slab for a few feet and traverse right to the obvious flake crack. Climb this and continue in the same line to the top of the crag.

Little Eastern 150 feet Very Severe (1964)
Below and to the right of Boomerang is a steep smooth wall bounded to the right by an obvious groove.
Start: Below the groove.
1 80 feet. Climb up to the groove. Follow this and the crack, moving right at the top, then left to a ledge.
2 70 feet. Move right into a flake chimney. Up this to a large grass ledge. Scramble off right.

The Far East Buttress

The Far East can be split into two sections, the Lower Far East and the Upper Far East. By far the best climbing is to be found on the left side of the upper section, on the buttress taken by Woubits and The Mostest, which gives steep climbing on reasonable rock. To the right of this buttress the cliff is split by three grooves but is somewhat loose. The lower section provides several routes, from Mostest Direct Start on the left, past the obvious break taken by Stomach Traverse, up to the slaty right hand section taken by Gormod and Land of Hope and Glory. The routes are described on the upper section and then on the lower section.

The routes on the Mostest buttress are best reached by descending the Far Eastern Terrace, which lies to the left of the buttress.

Brwynog Chimney 160 feet Very Severe (1933)
A good chimney climb in the classical idiom. Slightly wet and loose.
Start: Half way down the Far Eastern Terrace directly below the chimney.
1 60 feet. Climb the chimney until it falls back into a slabby formation, and go up the slab to an overhang. Chockstone belay on left.
2 100 feet. Step back into the chimney and go up to the slight overhang. Climb this and step into the crack on the right. Up this and the easy chimney above to the top.

* **The Key** 215 feet Mild Extremely Severe (1 pt. aid) (1965)
Start: As for Brwynog Chimney.
1 60 feet. As for Brwynog Chimney.
2 80 feet. Traverse right across the wall into the corner using a sling on a dubious spike for aid, past a protection peg. Climb the corner to a glacis, then up via ledges to a stance and belay.
3 75 feet. Step right and climb the groove to the top.

** **Sinistra** 260 feet Extremely Severe (1 pt. aid) (1965)
A good climb taking the wall on the left of Woubits.
Start: As for Woubits.
1 50 feet. As for Woubits to a stance and belay on a block forming an overhang.
2 85 feet. Climb up for 10 feet and left to a groove. Go horizontally left until it is possible to climb up into a grass-filled slot. Move left again round a rib and down to a good stance.
3 60 feet. With a shoulder for aid reach a large hold above the left

hand end of the ledge. Go up to a flake runner, then left to a small ledge and corner. Climb the right arête of the corner as for the Key, to a stance and belay.

4 65 feet. Climb the groove for 20 feet as for the Key. Step left into a smaller groove and climb this to the top.

* **Woubits Left Hand** 235 feet Extremely Severe (1959/*1975*)
An interesting climb with a very difficult last pitch.
Start: As for Woubits.

1 120 feet. As for Woubits.

2 65 feet. Move left and climb overhanging cracks and chimneys leftwards to a good stance.

3 50 feet. Climb the groove, past a protection peg near the top. Belay well back.

** **Woubits** 270 feet Extremely Severe (1955)
A difficult but good climb. It used to have a reputation for being loose and unprotected but this is no longer true. In the upper half it takes the prominent rightward curving groove.
Start: Almost at the foot of the terrace, below short twin grooves, directly below the upper grooves.

1 120 feet. Climb the overhang into the right hand of the twin grooves. Climb either of the grooves, the left one being much easier, and continue up the broken groove above. Move right to a stance and belay.

2 100 feet. Climb the groove above to a small overhang at 40 feet. Swing out left to a good flake and stand on this. Either mantelshelf onto a higher ledge and move back into the groove, or swing into the groove immediately. Continue up the easier groove to a constricted stance in the chimney.

3 50 feet. Step right and climb the slabby groove to the top.

** **The Mostest** 315 feet Mild Extremely Severe (1957)
A good route with an excellent second pitch in a fine position, although the route is slightly flawed by a poor first pitch. The difficulty is reserved for the final move of the third pitch, which can be impossible without aid in greasy conditions. Good protection throughout.
Start: Just right of Woubits, where the terrace fades into steeper rock.

1 120 feet. Up the grassy groove on the right and climb the slab with twin cracks. Continue up a short chimney to a grassy rake. Go left to a chimney-groove and up this to a cave stance and peg belay.

2 90 feet. Climb the crack on the left to the top of a pinnacle. Step right and go over the bulge to the wall on the right. Go up a few feet to a spike, descend a little, and follow the rising traverse line into the bottomless corner. Peg belay.

3 60 feet. Climb the corner to the overhang. Protection peg in the roof. Move left into another groove (hard) and climb up more easily to a stance.
4 45 feet. Climb the broken slab to the top.

Naddyn Ddu 270 feet Extremely Severe (2 pts. aid) (1962)
A poor route, loose and not worthwhile. Climbs the groove to the right of The Mostest.
Start: As for The Mostest.
1 50 feet. As for The Mostest to the first large grass ledge. Spike belay.
2 60 feet. Step right and go up a short groove. Continue up right to an overhanging crack to the right of the main groove. Up and right for 20 feet to belay on the grass pedestal.
3 100 feet. Up the overhanging crack for 40 feet. Tension down left from a peg to a line of holds leading into the groove (sling for aid). Climb up the steep wall until it is possible to step left to a sloping ledge where the crack in the groove starts. Up the groove to a ledge.
4 60 feet. Climb the groove and chimney to the top.

Variation
Direct Start 190 feet Extremely Severe (*1975*)
Climbs the wall below the main groove to join the normal route at the end of the tension traverse. Loose and even more pointless than the original route.
1a . 90 feet. As for Naddyn Ddu to the short groove on pitch 2. Go up the groove and scramble up left to belay below a pinnacle at the foot of the wall.
2a 100 feet. Start in the incipient groove on the left and climb up right to better holds. Continue up the wall past a very loose flake to a ledge. Two poor protection pegs in place. Continue up as for the normal route.

The Far East Girdle 435 feet. Mild Extremely Severe (2 pts. aid) (1965)
Start: As for Brwynog Chimney.
1 60 feet. As for Brwynog Chimney
2 80 feet. As for The Key.
3 100 feet. Traverse right along grass ledges to a peg and sling at foot level. Using the rope descend 40 feet and traverse right to the stance of Woubits.
4 45 feet. Move up and round the arête on the right. A descending traverse joins up with The Mostest. Follow this to belay at the foot of the corner.
5 90 feet. Up to the overhang, as for The Mostest. Move out right and up for 10 feet to a flake runner. Traverse right and descend a groove for 15 feet until it is possible to step right into Naddyn Ddu. Up

to a grass ledge and belay.
6 60 feet. Up the groove to the top.

The next five climbs start from the terrace of Jubilee and are best reached by climbing the first section of that route.

The Sceptre 170 feet Hard Very Severe (1956)
This climb takes the left hand of the three obvious breaks in the wall to the right of Mostest buttress. The 5-foot overhang is hard but the crack above is easy.
1 95 feet. Climb over the roof and up the crack to shattered pinnacles.
2 75 feet. Up the easy chimney and grassy corner.

* **The Orb** 190 feet Very Severe (1956)
A pleasant climb taking the centre of the three breaks.
1 20 feet. Up a thin crack in the wall and gain a ledge leading into the corner.
2 95 feet. Climb the corner. At 50 feet it eases and broken rock leads to shattered pinnacles on the left.
3 75 feet. Climb the chimney and corner as for The Sceptre.

The Bauble 150 feet Very Severe (1960)
Takes the break 30 feet right of The Orb. Loose and not recommended.
1 25 feet. Start as for The Orb but go right up a slanting crack in the wall. Move right into the bottom of the groove.
2 125 feet. Climb the loose groove to the top.

* **Slurp** 150 feet Hard Very Severe (1963)
A good route up the wall to the right of The Bauble on rather friable rock.
1 150 feet. Climb more or less straight up the steep wall right of The Bauble.

The Republican 390 feet Hard Very Severe (1972)
This route follows a natural traverse line, right to left, across the buttress.
Start: From the top of pitch 4 of Jubilee go steeply up and left to a peg belay a few feet below the overhanging band at the foot of the buttress, directly below a shallow grassy corner.
1 60 feet. Climb over the overhanging band on the left and climb a steep wall rightwards to the right end of a traverse line leading left. Belay at the edge of a gully.
2 120 feet. Traverse left along the obvious central weakness, rising slowly. Peg belay in a very shallow bay.
3 60 feet. Continue on the same line, crossing The Bauble. Move

up a little then go horizontally left into the corner of The Orb. Up this feet to a stance.

4 150 feet. Climb the corner for 15 feet and slant leftwards over huge pinnacles and blocks to the left arête of the buttress. Climb this to the top of the cliff.

The next few routes take lines up the lower band of rock on the Far East.

Rumplestiltskin 150 feet Mild Extremely Severe (1975)
Start: As for Mostest Direct Start.

1 150 feet. Climb the slaty slab slanting left to a ledge below the wall. Climb the wall to the prominent overhang and swing left round this to a slab under a larger overhang. Bridge up under the overhang until it is possible to swing right onto the wall. Climb this and the groove above.

Mostest Direct Start 200 feet Extremely Severe (*1957*)
A sustained pitch leading directly up to Mostest buttress.
Start: Directly below the foot of the Far Eastern Terrace on a small ridge.

1 150 feet. Climb easily up the ridge for a few feet. Traverse 10 feet right to a vague groove and climb this for 15 feet until forced out right. Climb up steeply until a grass ledge is reached below a corner. Climb this to easier ground.

2 50 feet. Scramble up the foot of The Mostest.

Chicane 200 feet Mild Extremely Severe (2 pts. aid) (1966)
About 50 feet right of Mostest Direct Start an obvious curving crack cuts the lower half of the buttress.
Start: Directly below this at the foot of easy slabs.

1 150 feet. Climb the crack to a protection peg in a short chimney at 80 feet. Move left and climb the overhang with a sling and a peg for aid, to a good ledge. Move left under a sharp rib and climb a short arête and chimney to a stance and peg belay on the right.

2 50 feet. Step down right and climb the obvious cracked chimney to easy ground.

Stomach Traverse 280 feet Extremely Severe (3 pts. aid) (1971)
A poor and unpleasant route taking the obvious diagonal break under the overhangs.
Start: Below the right hand end of the overhangs below a crack.

1 80 feet. Climb the crack or the rock on the right to a stance on the edge of a field.

2 120 feet. Climb across the wall below the overhangs to the obvious slot, which gives the first stomach traverse. Cross the undercut wall with 3 pegs for aid and follow the crack to finish along another stomach traverse. Spike belay 10 feet further left.

3 80 feet. Move back right along the traverse to a deep chimney. Climb this and the continuation cracks.

To the right is the big corner of Jubilee. The corner on the left of this has been climbed but is not particularly worthwhile.

Jubilee Climb 700 feet Severe (1935)

A long and tedious route which is difficult to follow and even more difficult to escape from. Not recommended as a route, but the first section provides a useful start to the climbs by The Sceptre. It starts up the obvious slanting groove to the right of the overhangs taken by Stomach Traverse and then traverses left across the large grass terrace and finishes up broken rocks at the left hand side of the upper tier. There are variations to pitches 7, 8, 9 and these can be useful if one gets lost. Jubilee Climb can be a good winter climb, given good snow conditions.

Start: Just to the left of the foot of the groove.

1 60 feet. Scramble across grass ledges to the crack in the back of the groove.

2 60 feet. Climb the crack to a thread belay.

3 50 feet. Continue up to a belay where the groove steepens.

4 60 feet. Climb the steep crack to a small ledge on the left. The slight bulge above is hard, then the groove falls back. Up easily to grass on the right.

5 60 feet. Scramble up grass slabs till they steepen.

6 25 feet. Climb the slab on the left, moving to the left, and go along the narrow grass ledge to a belay. Follow the large grass terrace for about 120 feet to its far end. Belay below a corner capped by a 5 foot overhang.

7 90 feet. Climb the slaty slab on the left and step round into the steep grass gully. Up this to the foot of an overhanging crack.

8 30 feet. Climb the crack and go easily up to a stance.

9 25 feet. Climb up past a chockstone.

10 120 feet. Climb up the loose gully to the top.

Route 68 300 feet Very Severe (1968)

Start: Directly below the groove of Jubilee.

1 90 feet. Traverse diagonally right into a leftward leaning shallow groove. Follow this to a grass ledge, move right on to a bulging nose and follow this to a grass pulpit on the left. Peg belay.

2 110 feet. Climb the shallow corner to the right until it is possible to step left into a corner with a crack in the back. Climb this moving left at the top to a grass ledge. Peg belay.

3 100 feet. Up the corner to the roof, move left and continue up the groove to the top.

* **Land of Hope and Glory** 300 feet Extremely Severe (1 pt. aid) (1971)

A good climb taking the left side of the prominent flake high in the centre of this section of cliff.

Start: About 80 feet left of Little Krapper, directly below the flake.

1 110 feet. Climb up trending left, then back right past a short slab. Climb the groove on the right of the slab to a niche. Exit right then back left to belay.

2 60 feet. Up for a few feet then left onto a ledge. Traverse left along this for 10 feet then climb the wall and a shallow groove to a ledge.

3 100 feet. Up right to the flake crack. Climb this with a peg for aid at the top, to a ledge. Up the clean groove moving left at the top and back right to a cracked block and up onto a short slab. Ledge and peg belay.

4 30 feet. Up the crack to the top.

Variation 160 feet Hard Very Severe

The original line, somewhat easier but still good.

Start: At the top of pitch 1.

2a 60 feet. Continue up the broken groove trending slightly right to the foot of an open corner with a steep left wall.

3a 100 feet. Climb the corner for a few feet and hand traverse left across the wall to the arête and a small ledge (the top of the flake crack) and continue up the clean groove as for pitch 3 above.

Gormod 220 feet Mild Extremely Severe (4 pts. aid) (1971)

Climbs up smooth rock with several points of aid. The name is Welsh for 'too much'.

Start: About 50 feet left of Little Krapper.

1 70 feet. Climb up and traverse left along a grass gangway. Climb back right across a slab into the groove. Go up to the overhang (protection peg) and move right and up to a ledge.

2 90 feet. Traverse left on the obvious line to reach a groove. Climb this with a peg for aid. Move left and then up with a peg for aid to the overhang. Move left using a sling for aid, then climb the overhanging groove above with a sling for aid. Peg belay.

3 60 feet. Move right and climb grassy grooves to the top.

* **Little Krapper** 200 feet Hard Very Severe (1963)

Good climbing up the attractive slabby rib starting just above the path. Protection is poor and the route is unfortunately easy to escape from.

1 150 feet. Climb up the rib, past one protection peg.

2 50 feet. Continue up to the top.

Camus 360 feet Severe (1955)
Climb the obvious chimney on the left of the upper part of East Gully. Scramble up to the start of the chimney then climb it direct. Loose and not recommended.

East Gully 500 feet Very Difficult (1912)
The lower section is just loose scrambling. The last 100 feet are steep and give two pitches of fairly easy but loose climbing. Not recommended as a climb but it can be descended to reach climbs on the Pinnacle. In winter it can give a good snow climb.

The Pinnacle

The Pinnacle has two distinct faces at right angles to each other. The wall overlooking East Gully is split by huge corners with undercut bases, up which most of the routes go. The front face, overlooking the East Buttress, is smoother, with the prominent capped groove of Taurus on the left and the Pinnacle Flake itself up on the right.

The rock in general is fairly good except at the level of the overhangs which guard the base all the way round. The approaches to some of the climbs are very loose and unpleasant. All the routes are steep and exposed but with good holds or good jamming cracks, and give much enjoyable climbing.

Beanlands 150 feet Hard Very Severe (1958)
A poor route which climbs the wall immediately right of East Gully. On the left of the amphitheatre below East Gully Wall is an overhanging crack.
Start: Below this.
1 60 feet. Traverse left on the obvious line to a rib. Up this to a stance on the right, virtually in East Gully.
2 20 feet. Traverse right round the steep arête via a flake to a tiny ledge below Moseley's Crack.
3 70 feet. Climb the crack behind the stance until it is possible to step into the deep crack on the right. Climb this.

* **East Gully Wall** 190 feet Mild Extremely Severe (1953)
A pleasant route, steep and well protected. The second pitch is considerably easier than the first pitch.
Start: At a pinnacle which leans against the overhangs about 150 feet right of the steep part of East Gully. The route goes across the steep wall and up the corner around to the left.
1 65 feet. Climb the crack on the left hand side of the pinnacle for about 10 feet. Move left for 15 feet to the foot of a thin crack. Climb this past a protection peg to a stance and peg belay.
2 85 feet. Make an ascending traverse to the arête. Step down and round the corner, past a loose flake, into the groove. Up this to a ledge and chock belay.
3 40 feet. Climb the corner.

Variations
Direct Start 120 feet Extremely Severe (2 pts. aid) *(1966)*
A strenuous and steep pitch. Often wet and then not worth doing.

Start: 40 feet right of East Gully at a pinnacle under a large overhang.
1a 120 feet. Climb the pinnacle and move right round the overhang into an overhanging groove with a peg for aid. Climb the groove to an overhang with a block jammed in it. Climb this with a sling for aid and continue up to join the normal route.

***Moseley's Variation** 125 feet Hard Very Severe (*1954*)
Start: From the top of pitch 1.
2a 55 feet. Make an ascending traverse to the arête on the left. Step down and round the corner to loose ledges on the left of the groove. Cross the ledges to a large flake and go up it to a stance in the corner.
3a 70 feet. Climb the crack in the corner to the top.

*****Shrike** 190 feet Mild Extremely Severe (1958)
A tremendous route with a sensational top pitch which climbs the steep wall on large holds. The first pitch is in common with East Gully Wall and is straightforward except for one very hard section.
Start: As for East Gully Wall.
1 65 feet. Climb the left side of the pinnacle for 10 feet, then traverse 15 feet left. Climb the thin crack, past a protection peg, to ledges and a peg belay.
2 125 feet. Climb the groove to a protection peg. Climb the overhang and wall above to where the crack widens. Gain ledges on the left, up a little, and traverse back to the crack on the obvious line. Up past two spike runners to a small ledge. Go left to the arête and climb this for a few feet then move right to a narrow ledge. Finish up the short wall above.

****East Gully Groove** 155 feet Very Severe (1953)
An excellent route giving VS climbing in HVS situations. Steep, exposed and enjoyable. The rock is sometimes doubtful.
Start: As for East Gully Wall.
1 90 feet. Climb the right hand side of the pinnacle to its top. Climb a shallow groove to the overhang. Swing right round the corner and up a sloping gangway into the main groove. Up this and take the overhang direct. Stance and belay just above.
2 65 feet. Up the groove to the top.

Variation
Direct Start 60 feet Mild Extremely Severe (*1957*)
A strenuous pitch up the lower part of the groove. Often wet.
1a 60 feet. Climb the crack and overhang to join the normal route.

The Croak 200 feet Mild Extremely Severe (1962)
A steep climb taking the buttress just right of East Gully Groove. The second half follows Pinnacle Girdle.

Start: As for Gargoyle.

1 40 feet. Traverse right for 25 feet, as for Gargoyle, to the top of a pedestal. Climb the wall above to a niche. Thread belay.

2 70 feet. Traverse left to the arête. Climb this for a few feet and traverse left into a groove. Go up this for 25 feet. Move right and climb the wall to ledges. Peg belay.

3 60 feet. Up the wall to an obvious traverse line. Traverse left to a protection peg and climb the wall above to a cave. Peg belay. (Pitch 7 of the Girdle).

4 30 feet. Move left and climb the very loose arête.

Easy Rider 190 feet Very Severe (1970)
Start: As for The Croak.

1 40 feet. As for The Croak.

2 70 feet. Climb the overlap on the right, then straight up the overhanging groove and the arête above to the ledges at the top of pitch 2 of The Croak.

3 80 feet. Climb the easy chimney on the right until the narrow buttress right of the chimney can be gained. Climb a wall and then a slab until the buttress steepens at the top. Traverse right, then climb the overhang and finish up a chimney.

Gargoyle 200 feet Hard Very Severe (1953)
The route starts below East Gully Groove and after a very loose traverse to the right, it takes the groove on the right of the Croak buttress finishing up the right hand of two chimneys.

1 40 feet. Traverse right descending slightly, on rotten rock, to a stance in the corner.

2 75 feet. Climb the crack and wide chimney to a stance.

3 25 feet. Scramble up into the bottom of the narrowing chimney.

4 60 feet. Climb the chimney direct, moving right at the top over doubtful rock.

Variation
Direct Start 120 feet Hard Very Severe (*1971*)
Good crack climbing. Below the main pitch of Gargoyle are two cracks a few feet apart. To the left from the foot of Octo is a large pinnacle belay.

1a 120 feet. Climb a rib on the left to a grassy slope below a cave. Protection peg at the back of this. Traverse right with difficulty on improving rock and climb the left hand crack.

* **Aries** 165 feet Very Severe (1965)
A good exposed route taking the obvious line of weakness across the smooth wall to the right of Gargoyle. The climbing is of a reasonable standard but there is not much of it.

1 40 feet. As for Gargoyle.
2 50 feet. Traverse right across the wall to a peg belay by loose blocks at the foot of a crack.
3 75 feet. Climb the crack and rock above to the top.

Octo 160 feet Hard Very Severe (1952) **
A good and imposing crack climb taking the crack on the right of the smooth wall crossed by Aries. The main pitch is strenuous but well protected.
Start: Scramble to the foot of the crack from the foot of Pinnacle Arête or from the East Gully. Both ways are unpleasant and dangerous.
1 50 feet. Climb either crack. The left one is better but harder. Stance in the chimney.
2 110 feet. Climb up to the overhang and up the crack above until it is possible to move out right. Easier climbing leads to the grass platform.

The Hand Traverse 120 feet Extremely Severe (1960) *
A short and sensationally exposed climb which traverses left across the wall above Aries with excellent incut holds. Strong fingers make it straightforward, otherwise it can be very intimidating.
Start: At the top of Octo.
1 100 feet. Step down and follow the obvious hand traverse for 20 feet to a protection peg. Move left and climb the thin crack and corner to a boulder bridge near the top.
2 20 feet. Continue to the top.

Pinnacle Arête 150 feet Mild Extremely Severe (1962) **
An excellent climb in a good position which takes the arête between the two main faces on the Pinnacle.
Start: As for Taurus.
1 130 feet. Follow Taurus for 30 feet and traverse left on flakes to a ledge on the arête. Go up to an old protection peg and move onto the arête proper. Climb a thin crack to a loose spike. Traverse left for 15 feet to a groove and climb it to a ledge and peg belays.
2 20 feet. Up to the top.

Taurus 130 feet Extremely Severe (1956)
A difficult and strenuous pitch, which gets harder as one gets higher. Protection is reasonable. The climb takes the obvious groove capped by an overhang on the left hand side of the front face of the Pinnacle.
Start: Scramble up loose rock to the foot of the groove.
1 130 feet. Climb up to the overhang. Turn it on the left and climb the groove above, then pull over the small overhang to a ledge on the right. Climb the thin crack on the right of the next overhang to ledges and the top.

* **Spillikin** 135 feet Hard Very Severe (1952)
An enjoyable climb which climbs the exposed wall to the right of Taurus.
Start: At the foot of Taurus.
1 100 feet. Climb the wall to a ledge on the arête. It is possible to take a poor belay here. Continue up in a direct line until a step can be made into a shallow groove. Go up this to a stance.
2 35 feet. Traverse along the ledge on the right and so up to the Meadow.

Guinivere 130 feet Hard Very Severe (1960)
The main value of this route is as a first pitch to the Girdle. Starting from below the Direct Finish to the East Buttress it traverses the front face of the Pinnacle to finish up the left side of the Pinnacle Flake.
1 70 feet. Step round the arête as low as possible and move up to the sloping ledge of Pinnacle Flake. Traverse across to a protection peg at foot level and step down and across to a short corner. Up this to a small stance and chock belay.
2 60 feet. Climb the corner for 10 feet to a ledge. Cross the steep wall to the base of the Flake and go up the crack on its left side to ledges. Scramble to the top.

* **Pinnacle Flake** 175 feet Mild Extremely Severe (1952)
The difficulty is unfortunately short-lived but the main pitch is exposed and in a fine position.
Start: As for the Direct Finish to the East Buttress.
1 85 feet. Climb up onto a sloping ledge on the aréte. Move up and left to a good ledge. Climb the crack on the right of the flake to a belay on its top.
2 90 feet. Move right to the arête and climb this to the top. Or climb up just left of the arête.

* **The Spire** 200 feet Mild Extremely Severe (1975)
Sustained climbing in a fine position up the right arête of the front face of the Pinnacle.
Start: Under the obvious niches at the foot of the face. Peg belay.
1 75 feet. Climb into a niche up on the left and then move out right into another niche. Climb out left and move up to join Pinnacle Flake. Follow this to the good ledge and move left and belay at the foot of the crack up the Flake.
2 125 feet. Go back to the arête and climb a shallow groove to reach better holds. Continue up until forced onto the right wall. Up this for 10 feet then step back left onto a ledge. Continue up the arête to the top.

Direct Finish to the East Buttress 180 feet Hard Severe (1932)
A pleasant but slight pitch. Takes the obvious corner on the right of

the Pinnacle Face. Scramble to its foot. Peg belay.
1 40 feet. Climb the corner to a good stance and belay, past some tricky mantelshelves.
2 100 feet. Up more easily to a good stance at 100 feet.
3 40 feet. Climb up a few feet then break out on to the left wall.

** **The Pinnacle Girdle** 590 feet Extremely Severe (1961)
A superb route with good climbing and some of the best positions on the cliff. It is strenuous and sustained at a high standard, with a gripping abseil down an overhanging arête high above the ground.
Start: As for Guinivere.
1 80 feet. Pull round and up to a ledge on the arête. Traverse left to a protection peg at foot level. Step down and across to a shallow corner. Climb this to a protection peg at the top on the left and climb down and across to a ledge on Spillikin. Peg belay.
2 60 feet. Go up the arête on the left and traverse into Taurus below the roof. Turn this on the left and climb the groove to a ledge and peg belay on the right.
3 80 feet. Climb the groove on the left for 10 feet and move left to a ledge past a protection peg. Step across to the arête and continue round at the same level to a ledge at the start of The Hand Traverse.
4 60 feet. Traverse left for 20 feet along the obvious line of The Hand Traverse to a protection peg. Move left and climb the thin crack to belay at the foot of the groove.
5 70 feet. Climb the groove for a few feet. Traverse left to a protection peg on the arête. Step across the shallow groove and go down slightly and across to the arête of Gargoyle. Up this for a few feet and step across to belay.
6 50 feet. Climb down Gargoyle for 30 feet and step left to ledges. Go up these to below an easy chimney on the right.
7 60 feet. Climb up to the obvious traverse line. Traverse left for 20 feet, protection peg. Climb the wall above to a cave stance and peg belay.
8 50 feet. Move left to the arête. Make a diagonal abseil into East Gully Groove via a thread runner on the end of the large flake.
9 80 feet. Step left and go up a thin crack for 15 feet. Move left rising slightly and go across to the large spike on Shrike. Move left to the arête, up a few feet, then back right and climb the wall above to the top.

The East Buttress

The East Buttress is almost a perfect triangular shape. The steep wall of East Gully defines the vertical side and the slabby syncline of the Eastern Terrace gives the hypotenuse. A grass break, that of Green Gallery, runs horizontally across it at half height, dividing the lower part, the East Buttress proper, from the upper part, the Pinnacle.

All the climbs on the East are very steep, and therefore strenuous, and very exposed. Most of the climbs follow crack lines, giving mainly jamming and bridging techniques, but some of them take the very steep walls between the cracks, to give some of the best climbing on the cliff. The rock is very sound all over the buttress and there is little grass, except on ledges, which doesn't really matter.

The first major break on the left is a deep crack facing left, Sunset Crack. Then comes a very large steep wall with two prominent grooves in its upper part, up which Serth and Llithrig finish. The next major break, that of Pigott's is composed of huge blocks stuck on the cliff and slanting to the right. On the right of Pigott's is the obvious line of Chimney Route, going straight up the buttress, and facing left as do nearly all the East Buttress cracks. On the right hand side of the vast central wall is a face crack running straight up the buttress. This is November, and Vember takes the parallel crack starting from the grass rake half way up. To the right of this is a huge flake of rock, curving in its upper half, giving Curving Crack on its left and the straight Pedestal Crack on its right. Troach finds its way up the outside of the flake, and Scorpio climbs the face to the right of Pedestal. The last major feature on the East is that of The Corner, a very obvious Cenotaph-like corner, and to the right of this the buttress tapers into the ground, with a few short cracks.

If time and inclination allow it is a good idea to finish up one of the Pinnacle Face routes. Otherwise the best way off from all the routes is to traverse the Green Gallery to the Eastern Terrace. It is possible to descend the rocks in East Gully to the left of Sunset, but they are loose and dangerous. The Eastern Terrace is easy if one keeps close under the Boulder where it narrows to a gully, and then back over the Middle Rock to the foot of the East again.

***Sunset Crack** 180 feet Very Severe (1937)
A steep, interesting and well protected climb. It takes the first major feature on the East, a steep chimney crack facing left.

Start: Scramble up to the foot of the crack.
1 20 feet. Easily up to a grass ledge. Belay on the left.
2 25 feet. Traverse diagonally right into the crack and climb it for a few feet to a good stance.
3 65 feet. Continue up the crack. Belay on the left below the overhang.
4 50 feet. Climb up a few feet, either in the narrow chimney or on the left wall. Continue up the easier corner to an easy rake. Belay at the foot of a short chimney.
5 20 feet. Climb the short easy chimney to the Green Gallery.

The broken wall on the left of Sunset gives a series of short pitches.

** **Serth** 210 feet Extremely Severe (1961)
A superb route taking a slightly artificial line up grooves in the arête between Sunset and Llithrig. The name is Welsh for "steep".
Start: By scrambling to the foot of Sunset.
1 90 feet. Scramble up to the right to short twin grooves and climb these to a junction with Llithrig. Follow this for a few feet until it is possible to traverse left into the bottom of a shallow slanting groove almost on the arête of Sunset. Climb the groove to a sloping ledge and continue to a better ledge.
2 80 feet. Descend to the sloping ledge and move right to a diagonal quartz break. Climb up into the obvious groove above and climb it to grass ledges.
3 40 feet. Up the cracked wall and flake on the right.

* **The Leech** 270 feet Extremely Severe (1971)
A difficult and fingery route taking a direct line up to the final groove of Serth. The second pitch is good although short.
Start: By a spring below the final groove of Serth.
1 75 feet. Climb the short buttress via a shallow scoop which is gained by a diagonal crack on the left. Belay on the grass ledge.
2 65 feet. Climb the obvious groove past a protection peg to the overhang on Llithrig. Follow Llithrig up right to the spike where it is possible to swing right to a peg belay as for Llithrig.
3 130 feet. Regain the spike and traverse left to a blunt arête. Climb up and slightly left on small pockets to the quartz break below the final groove of Serth. Climb up to the groove and finish up this.

Variation
Direct Finish 120 feet Extremely Severe (*1975*)
3a 120 feet. Swing back left and climb directly up the obvious line above to reach the final crack of Llithrig. Finish up this.

**** Llithrig** 245 feet Hard Very Severe (1 pt. aid) (1952)
A very good route with thin sustained climbing at a reasonable standard, and an interesting rope move. Starting from Sunset it traverses into the middle of the steep wall on the right and goes straight up this.
1 45 feet. The first two pitches of Sunset.
2 70 feet. Traverse across the wall into a shallow groove and go up this for a few feet to a small ledge on the arête. Traverse right into the corner. Climb the overhang and diagonal break to a good spike. Pendulum across right to a ledge and peg belay.
3 70 feet. Traverse right and climb the obvious break to a stance.
4 40 feet. Climb the corner for 15 feet. Traverse left to a crack and go up this to better holds on the left wall leading to a large grass stance. Or climb the corner direct.
5 20 feet. Up the wall behind.

*** Capricorn** 360 feet Mild Extremely Severe (1973/*1975*)
A very contrived route taking a wandering line between Llithrig and Pigott's, although the climbing is good. The final pitch takes a fine steep crack giving very hard but good climbing.
1 60 feet. As for Pigott's.
2 100 feet. Climb a faint groove left of Pigott's to a layback flake. Up this and left to the stance of Llithrig.
3 110 feet. Follow Llithrig for 30 feet then follow a line of flakes right into Pigott's below the corner.
4 90 feet. Climb the thin crack in the wall left of Pigott's, past three protection pegs.

Pigott's Climb 270 feet Very Severe (1927)
Poor initial pitches lead to the final steep corner which gives strenuous climbing although the hard sections can be missed out on the right. Worth doing for the air of tradition. The next break right of Sunset slants right and is composed of enormous blocks resting on the cliff. The route traverses right to these from the left and then goes up vertical corners.
Start: By a mossy spring.
1 60 feet. Up grassy ledges for 40 feet. Climb a steep groove to a good ledge and belays on the left.
2 50 feet. From the right hand end of the ledge climb a steep rib, then traverse right to the foot of a short steep corner. Climb this to a broad grass ledge, the Conservatory.
3 70 feet. Up the corner easily but steeply. From the ledge on the right at 50 feet climb the chimney to the top of a massive pillar.
4 90 feet. Climb directly up the corners to the top.

Variations

4a 60 feet. Climb the corner to a sloping ledge. Move up to another ledge and climb a subsidiary crack to a good ledge.

5a 30 feet. Climb the thin crack on the right of the corner.

5b 30 feet. Traverse round the corner on the right and go up the left hand of two grooves.

Wall Variations 280 feet Mild Extremely Severe

A poor route taking the rock between Pigott's and Chimney. Not really worthwhile. After the first two pitches the climbing is VS (The Wall Finish to Pigott's.

Start: By a pinnacle below the Conservatory.

1 70 feet. Climb up to a thin crack in the left side of the small face. Up this to the Conservatory.

2 80 feet. Traverse right under the overhang to an obvious crack. Climb this and continue to a stance by the massive pillar on Pigott's.

3 60 feet. Go diagonally right for 30 feet and climb the broken wall above to a stance.

4 70 feet. Traverse right along a ledge to Chimney Route. Up the Crooked Finish to the top.

Trapeze 250 feet Extremely Severe (3 pts. aid) (1965)

Takes the overhang to the right of Wall Variations.

Start: 20 feet left of Chimney.

1 30 feet. Climb the green corner, stepping right at the top to a ledge and flake belay.

2 80 feet. Move left to a slab and climb this to the bulge. Go over this with 3 points of aid and continue to the horizontal break. Traverse right to a ledge and peg belay.

3 70 feet. Traverse right for 15 feet to an obvious line up the wall. Climb this until a step left can be made into a shallow groove. Up this, past a protection peg, to a horizontal break. Step left and go up to a triangular grass ledge.

4 70 feet. Up the corner above and continue up the first groove, past a protection peg, until it joins the variation finish to Pigott's.

* **The Sweeper** 250 feet Mild Extremely Severe (1975)

A good and very well protected climb taking the thin crack in the wall to the left of Chimney Route.

1 60 feet. As for Chimney.

2 130 feet. Follow Chimney for 6 feet then move left to the thin crack. Climb this until it is possible to step right into a small niche below small roofs. Surmount these, move left, then up a steep slab rightwards to a good belay ledge.

3 60 feet. Climb the groove behind the belay then move right into another groove. Up this into a niche, then leftwards to the top.

** **Chimney Route** 250 feet Very Severe (1931)
A good route, with the chimney sections best climbed by bridging. Due to the dangerous state of the top overhang the route is described with the Diglyph finish, which provides a strong contrast to the initial pitches.
Start: Almost in the centre of the East is an obvious chimney line bounding the large central wall on the left. Scramble up to the foot of the chimney.
1 60 feet. Climb the wall on the right to a good stance in the chimney. Or climb the chimney.
2 50 feet. Continue up for 30 feet until one is forced right. Continue up on good holds until the chimney reappears.
3 60 feet. Up for 45 feet to where the right wall falls back into a slab. Up this to a peg belay.
4 80 feet. Climb down right and step round the arête into a groove. Climb this to a large flake. Traverse right and climb the steep wall on good holds to the Green Gallery. A very exposed pitch. Scramble off to the left, or finish up Continuation Chimney.
5 110 feet. The Continuation Chimney. Climb the obvious chimney in the corner.

Variations.
4a 60 feet. The Rickety Innards. Climb the overhang above, which is in very poor condition, and continue to the top. Not recommended.
4b 70 feet. The Crooked Finish. From just above the stance traverse left to a good ledge. Climb up to the ledge above. Traverse back into the chimney above the overhang and continue up to the top

* **Diglyph** 260 feet Hard Very Severe (1951)
A technically interesting climb taking the crack in the right wall of chimney. This is strenuous, well protected and hard to start. The top pitch gives easier climbing in an exposed position overlooking Great Wall.
1 60 feet. As for Chimney.
2 90 feet. Traverse 10 feet right and climb the crack to the top, past a protection peg at the bulge just above a small ledge. Belay at far end of ledge.
3 110 feet. Climb up to the obvious groove. Follow it for 80 feet until it steepens at a large flake. Move right and climb the steep wall to the top. The groove can be climbed direct but is harder and not as good.

* **Daurigol** 270 feet Extremely Severe (1962)
A very hard and technical climb taking the grooves on the left side of Great Wall.

Start: Below these.
1 80 feet. Climb diagonally left to a horizontal quartz break by a small roof. Move right and up to a stance.
2 80 feet. Move right to the groove. Climb this until holds lead left into the second groove. Climb this to belay as for Diglyph.
3 110 feet. As for Diglyph.

*****Great Wall** 230 feet Hard Extremely Severe (1962/*1975*)
A magnificent route of great difficulty and exposure which follows the thin crack in the left side of the large central wall. Since the first ascent the aid on this route has been gradually eliminated and the climb is now described in its free state. It is probably the hardest and one of the best climbs on the cliff.
Start: Just right of the thin crack.
1 80 feet. Climb diagonally left to a small overhang at 20 feet. Climb the crack and groove above, past a protection peg, to another crack. Up this, past a protection peg, to a peg belay where the angle eases.
2 150 feet. Continue up for 40 feet to a thin crack. Climb this to a very small corner. Move up and right past a poor protection peg to a ledge. Traverse right then back left and up easier ground to belay at the foot of Continuation Chimney.

A variation start to Great Wall has been climbed utilising 4 pegs and a bolt.

***The Arête Finish** 115 feet Mild Extremely Severe (*1966*)
To the right of Continuation Chimney is a steep arête which gives a good but poorly protected pitch in a fine exposed position.
1 115 feet. Traverse right from Continuation Chimney and climb up to a protection peg. Continue up and into a crack to finish.

Blancmange Sandwich 120 feet Extremely Severe (1975)
A very difficult and sustained climb taking the left hand of the two grooves above Great Wall. A steep pitch.
Start: 15 feet left of the corner below a small groove.
1 120 feet. Climb the groove to good handholds. Traverse right into
* the corner and go up to the sloping ledge. Climb diagonally left across the wall and then back right on good handholds into the groove. Continue directly up this with difficulty. Good belays well back.

****Jelly Roll** 290 feet Extremely Severe (1971)
An excellent route which takes the right hand groove above Great Wall.
1 90 feet. As for November.
2 70 feet. As for November until the crack closes. Go left to a hidden flake crack and climb this to a grass ledge.

3 130 feet. Climb the groove, taking the final overhang by a crack on its left.

* **November** 380 feet Extremely Severe (1957/*1970*)
A very direct and obvious line up steep rock with a sustained and strenuous crux pitch, and fine situations.
Start: At the obvious wide crack just left of the pedestal of Curving Crack.
1 110 feet. Climb the crack for 90 feet. Go up the ramp on the right to belay.
2 150 feet. Descend the ramp and continue up the crack to a large grass ledge. Belay at the back.
3 120 feet. Climb the corner and continuation cracks to the top.

** **Vember** 310 feet Mild Extremely Severe (1951)
A very fine and exposed route, sustained at a high level of technical interest, but with good protection on the main pitch. It shares the first pitch with November and then takes a parallel crack to the right.
1 110 feet. Climb the crack for 90 feet, then go up the ramp on the right to the foot of an obvious crack.
2 120 feet. Climb the crack and the groove above, with a protection peg just below the short V-chimney. Belay at the back of the large grass ledge.
3 80 feet. Climb up the right wall of the corner and up the cracks.

Medi 150 feet Extremely Severe (1 pt. aid) (1975)
A serious route, very steep and sustained, with some doubtful rock in places. It takes the thin crack between Vember and Curving Crack.
Start: At the top of pitch 1 of Vember, beneath a crack to the right of Vember.
1 150 feet. Climb the crack above trending right to a peg at 30 feet. Tension rightwards across the wall to a long thin flake. Follow this into the steep crack. Climb this with difficulty until it is possible to gain a niche on the right. Good nut on the left here. Move left and climb the faint crack and continue to the top.

* **Curving Crack** 205 feet Very Severe (1932)
A very good climb, enjoyment being proportional to one's chimneying technique. The climb is in three distinct parts; a thin crack, a chimney, and a steep slab.
Start: To the right of the smooth central wall is a deep crack which curves to the right in its upper half. Start at the right hand side of the pedestal at the foot of the main crack. This is reached via an easy slab.
1 35 feet. Climb the crack to a ledge.
2 60 feet. Swing left into the main crack on a good hold and go up to belay on a ledge on the left.

3 110 feet. Climb the crack until the angle eases. Climb the arête and slabs to the top.

Variation

Direct Start 30 feet Very Severe

1a 30 feet. Climb the crack on the left hand side of the pedestal. Harder and dirtier.

Curving Arête 205 feet Hard Extremely Severe (1971)

A very serious route with poor protection, taking the obvious arête to the right of Curving Crack.

1 65 feet. As for Curving Crack to a chockstone belay in the chimney, where it is possible to move right to the arête.

2 140 feet. Go out to the arête, and climb it and the easier angled arête above to the top.

** **Troach** 210 feet Extremely Severe (1959)

An excellent route up the steep wall on the right of Curving Crack. The difficulty is not great except for a strenuous start and a thin crux. Nicely exposed.

1 35 feet. As for Curving Crack to the ledge.

2 120 feet. Move right and up onto the quartz ledge. Follow the good holds up, past a protection peg, to another protection peg under a small overhang. Go right and up to a large flake belay.

3 55 feet. Follow the line of holds diagonally left to the arête. Up this to the top.

** **Pedestal Crack** 175 feet Very Severe (1931/*1932*)

A pleasant route, steep and exposed, with good jamming and protection. Hard for its grade. Takes the obvious crack to the right of Curving.

Start: Below this.

1 50 feet. Climb the crack. Belay on the right on top of the Pedestal.

2 30 feet. Continue up the crack to a stance in the corner.

3 95 feet. Continue up to the top.

Variation

The Original Start

1a 60 feet. Climb the rib on the right of the crack; much easier.

** **Scorpio** 130 feet Extremely Severe (1961)

A very good and varied climb, continuously difficult and strenuous, which takes the wall to the right of Pedestal. The top moves are quite bold, although no harder than moves below.

Start: From the top of the Pedestal, gained by climbing the rib right of Pedestal Crack (Pitch 1a of that climb).

1 130 feet. From the right hand end of the ledge, climb a shallow groove to the hand traverse line. Thread runner. Go right for 20 feet and up to a ledge. Climb the groove to a small overhang. Move left and up to a protection peg, and go right to a blind flake crack. Climb this and a short wall to the top.

* **Silhouette** 170 feet Extremely Severe (1975)
A difficult route which climbs the obvious thin crack up the wall of Scorpio, following Scorpio in the middle section.
Start: Left of The Corner.
1 50 feet. Climb the thin crack to the short groove on Scorpio. Nut and flake belay.
2 120 feet. Climb the groove, move left and go up to a protection peg (as for Scorpio). Continue up the crack to a small roof. Climb over this and continue up the crack to the top.

** **The Corner** 120 feet Hard Very Severe (1952)
An excellent pitch, long and strenuous. Good protection makes this a fine route to get fit on.
Start: Directly below the obvious corner, gained by climbing the rib to the right of Pedestal Crack or up ledges directly below the corner.
1 120 feet. Climb the corner to the top, moving out onto the left wall at about 20 feet.

* **The Shadow** 190 feet Extremely Severe (1962)
An excellent route with a superb but short middle pitch. The pitch is not too well protected and has one very hard move.
Start: Directly below the blunt arête on the right of The Corner.
1 80 feet. Climb a shallow groove and twin cracks until one can move right to a stance and nut belay below the first overhang.
2 70 feet. Go up a shallow groove on the left for 20 feet. Move right and climb the wall, past a protection peg, to the overhang. Take it on the right and climb the groove to a ledge. Small flake belays.
3 40 feet. Move right for several feet onto a ramp. Up this to the top.

Mordor 150 feet Extremely Severe (3 pts. aid) (1969)
A difficult climb which takes the thin crack to the right of Shadow.
Start: Below the crack. Peg belay.
1 150 feet. Climb the groove to a protection peg under the roof. Climb the thin crack to the top with two nuts and a peg for aid.

Terrace Crack 150 feet Very Severe (1931)
A slight but pleasant route. To the right of Mordor are prominent twin cracks a few feet apart.
Start: In a corner just above the path and below the cracks.

1 30 feet. Climb the crack and ledges on the right to a belay.
2 35 feet. Climb the groove above. Belay below the left hand crack.
3 85 feet. Climb the crack for 35 feet, move left and back into the chimney. Climb this or its left ledge to the top.

The East Buttress Girdle 830 feet Hard Very Severe (1 pt. aid) (1953)
An interesting route with character and exposure, and a frightening abseil down Jelly Roll.
Start: As for Sunset.
1 45 feet. As for Sunset. Go up the wall and traverse right into the crack.
2 70 feet. As for Llithrig. Traverse across the wall into a shallow groove and go up this to a small ledge on the arête. Traverse right to a corner and climb the overhang and diagonal break to a good spike. Pendulum right to a ledge. Peg belay.
3 70 feet. Traverse right into Pigott's. Climb the chimney to the massive pillar.
4 80 feet. Traverse right under the nose and climb the wall on the right to a long ledge. Go along this. Climb down into Chimney Route.
5 70 feet. Make a descending traverse to the right and round the arête into the groove of Diglyph. Climb this to a large flake. Traverse right and down to a grassy corner.
6 85 feet. Go down the crack on the right and make a long descending traverse to the right, then ascend a system of grooves and ledges on the right to belay on the grass ledge below Jelly Roll.
7 95 feet. Abseil down to the ramp on Vember from a large flake on the right. Up the ramp to belay.
8 65 feet. Climb Curving Crack to a stance on the slab on the right.
9 20 feet. Step up and traverse around into Pedestal Crack.
10 100 feet. Abseil to the top of the Pedestal.
11 130 feet. Descend a little and make a rising traverse into The Corner. Finish up this.

The Middle Rock

Below the bottom of the Eastern Terrace is a subsidiary buttress, the Middle Rock, with a wet cave at its left hand end. It is steep and ribbed with vertical grooves, and rises up some 200 feet to a gentle shoulder of grass below the Boulder. There are three major grooves which give all the routes.

Moonshine 215 feet Hard Very Severe (1957)
The left hand of the three obvious grooves.
Start: Directly below it.
1 40 feet. Up to a stance about 20 feet below the corner proper.
2 100 feet. Up to the corner and climb this to the overhang at 70 feet. Traverse left to a grass ledge. Belay further left.
3 75 feet. Climb the shattered chimney and its overhang. Traverse right and go up the corner.

Variation
Direct Finish 150 feet Hard Very Severe (1 pt. aid) (*1966*)
2a 150 feet. As for pitch 2 to the overhang at 70 feet. Climb over this with a peg for aid and continue to the top.

Birthday Crack 200 feet Very Severe (1932)
A pleasant climb taking the middle groove.
Start: Just to the right of the line of the groove.
1 90 feet. Climb up and left, avoiding difficulties by moving left. Constricted stance in the bottom of the groove.
2 110 feet. Climb the groove until it is possible to step right to a good hold. Up grass to finish.

Bridge Groove 130 feet Very Severe (1931)
1 130 feet. Climb the right hand of the three grooves.

The shallow groove on the right can also be climbed at a similar standard.

The West Buttress

The West Buttress is of complicated slab and corner formation. It is bounded on its left by the Eastern Terrace, and at its base by the Western Terrace, which slants up to meet the summit ridge. The base of the buttress is guarded by enormous overhangs which make most climbs difficult of entry. A separate facet of the buttress, on the left, directly above the Middle Rock, is called the Boulder. This is separated from the West proper by a very obvious straight, black, wet groove, the Black Cleft.

The rock in general is good and tends to be flaky, thus giving climbing of a delicate nature, but it deteriorates very much at the level of the overhangs and towards the right hand side of the buttress. There is a lot of grass, which spoils one or two routes and keeps the buttress wet for longer than usual. However there is little grass on the harder routes and it is gradually being removed from the others.

The first break to the right of the Black Cleft is a narrow slab with an over-arching right wall, the typical structure of the West; this is Longland's. The next obvious feature is an hourglass-shaped slab, light in colour, the White Slab.

Nestling between this and Longland's is the slender line of Ghecko Groove, with its distinct widening at half height. Then comes a vertical system of ribs and grooves, up which Sheaf finds its way, bounded on its right by the obvious Narrow Slab. To the right of this is the vast central mass of the Great Slab, with its Bow-Shaped scoop in its left hand side. The Great Slab, like its slender sisters, ends with a corner, Moss Groove, and an overhanging wall which gives hard definition to Central Rib. Beyond this the buttress is more broken, but still shows slab and grooves at a slightly easier angle. Bloody Slab is obvious by its colour and the large overhangs above; the next slab is grassy, the Carpet Slab. Then the buttress tapers off into the ridge with large areas of broken rock and grass.

Climbs starting at the left hand end are best reached by scrambling over the Middle Rock and down to the foot of the Eastern Terrace, thus avoiding the unpleasant rocks below. Both the Eastern and the Western Terrace provide convenient descents.

Prominus 120 feet Very Severe (1973)
Climbs the obvious hanging slab up the Eastern Terrace from the

Boulder.

1 60 feet. Using a large hold gain the overhanging prow at the foot of the slab. Move up to a block and step right along the lip of the overhang to reach easier angled rock. Up this to belay in a recess.

2 60 feet. Follow the obvious rake up left to a wall. Traverse back right above the belay and climb a short wall to the top.

Adam's Rib 200 feet Very Severe (1973)

To the left of East Wall Climb is a prominent right-angled corner with a crack in the angle.

Start: Below this.

1 70 feet. Climb the corner crack for 40 feet. Follow its continuation diagonally right to ledges. Move left under the rib to a belay in a small grassy bay.

2 50 feet. Move down right and climb the rib to a grassy ledge. Diagonally left up grass to belay at a large boulder.

3 80 feet. Move down right and climb the continuation rib. At half height move round to the right and finish up a crack.

East Wall Climb 90 feet Very Difficult (1905)

A very short and pointless climb. Starts above the short gully section of the Eastern Terrace and follows an obvious break in the wall.

Start: From the Terrace a few yards above the cave.

1 25 feet. Climb a steep little rib on the left of the main break to ledge at 20 feet. Turn right into the corner. Or reach the ledge by a traverse from the left, harder.

2 40 feet. Climb a short wall to a chimney. Up this and leave it behind the chockstone.

3 20 feet. Step left, and climb the easy crack. The difficulties are now over and the break continues as a scree filled gully to the top.

Flintstone Wall 170 feet Hard Very Severe (1970)

Climbs the left wall of the Boulder.

Start: Just left of Left Edge.

1 70 feet. Follow on ascending traverse line leftwards for 20 feet onto the steep face until one comes to a vague crack. Climb this for 20 feet then bear back right and climb the wall (crux of Left Edge) to a ledge. Peg belay.

2 100 feet. Traverse leftward to a fine groove. Climb this. Belay on a loose ledge on the right. Scrambling remains to the top.

Illegal Eagle 300 feet Hard Very Severe (1974)

Takes the obvious groove between Flintstone Wall and Left Edge.

Start: Left of these, at the lower end of the cave, below a bulging wall.

1 50 feet. Climb the wall and continue to a small pedestal.

Traverse left for 10 feet to a shallow crack, then diagonally up right to a ledge. Climb up to another ledge and traverse left to a crack. Follow this over a bulge and continue up the groove to a grass platform.
2 150 feet. Climb the easy chimney and continue by loose scrambling to the top.

* **Left Edge** 320 feet Hard Very Severe (1954)
A good route taking the left edge of the main face of the Boulder. The difficulties depend on the line taken and the route is not well protected.
Start: At an obvious break directly below the edge.
1 40 feet. Climb up to a small stance and peg belay.
2 130 feet. Step around the edge on the left and go up to a ledge at 30 feet. Climb the wall above (crux) to a ledge. Step right onto the front of the Boulder and go up a little then back left and up a groove on the edge to a grass rake. Up this to belay.
3 150 feet. Up grass to the top.

*** **The Boulder** 360 feet Hard Very Severe (1951)
A very fine pitch, exposed and poorly protected, which traverses across the front face of the Boulder.
1 40 feet. As for Left Edge.
2 130 feet. A long rising traverse leads away to the right. Gain it with difficulty and follow it for 30 feet. Mantelshelf onto a higher traverse line and continue right past a smooth scoop to good holds leading up to a stance and flake belay just beside the Black Cleft.
3 40 feet. Swing into the Black Cleft and go up to the overhang. Swing left to a ledge and climb the second part of the overhang by a shattered crack. Belay immediately.
4 150 feet. Climb up the grass gully to the top.

Variation Finish
3a 45 feet. Avoid the overhanging crack by traversing across the slab on the left and then go up in a straight line.

* **Gemini** 250 feet Extremely Severe (1970)
A difficult and poorly protected route up the face left of The Boldest. Slightly harder than, but not as good as, The Boldest.
Start: 20 feet left of The Boldest below a shallow groove.
1 110 feet. Climb the groove to a small ledge. Go left and up to a shallow groove. Protection peg. Step left and climb up to The Boulder traverse. Peg belay a few feet higher.
2 140 feet. Climb up a few feet to a protection peg and continue to a small ledge below a small roof. Traverse 20 feet left to a groove and protection peg. Climb the groove to the top.

***__The Boldest__** 150 feet Extremely Severe (1963)
A superb pitch, sustained and not well protected. The difficulty is continuous although not excessive, but the exposure makes the lack of protection felt.
Start: On the left of the obvious groove in the lower right part of the Boulder.
1 150 feet. Traverse into the groove and climb it to a large flake. Move right on to the arête and go up to the level of the overhang. Protection peg. Traverse left under the overhang to a small ledge. Climb the wall above, trending slightly left to reach a shallow depression. Traverse right and go up onto a small flake. Move up for a few feet then climb diagonally left to reach The Boulder traverse. Peg belay a few feet higher.

Variation
Direct Finish 70 feet Extremely Severe *(1969)*
2 70 feet. Climb the wall above, finishing up a shallow groove.

** **The Black Cleft** 360 feet Mild Extremely Severe (1952)
A very fine route with much interesting climbing. Unfortunately the route is always wet and so is climbed less frequently than it deserves. The two main pitches are sustained and are graded for wet conditions. The route takes the obvious corner dividing the Boulder from the West Buttress. Very well protected.
1 40 feet. At the foot of the corner is a pillar about 40 feet high. Climb its right hand side to a stance on the top or climb the crack on the left side, or the slab on the left of this. Both harder.
2 60 feet. Climb the corner to a small stance.
3 70 feet. Continue up to the first overhang. Climb this by a crack on the right and follow the groove above to a stance and flake belay. Junction with The Boulder.
4 40 feet. Climb the corner up to the overhang. Swing left to a ledge and climb the second part of the overhang by a shattered crack. Belay immediately.
5 150 feet. Up the gully to the top.

* **Longland's Climb** 340 feet Very Severe (1928)
A varied and exposed route with a distinct feeling of seriousness on the first two pitches, although the standard of the climbing is not too high. The climb follows the first slab on the West Buttress proper, which is reached by scrambling across to the foot of the slab from the foot of the Boulder.
1 90 feet. Climb the slab and corner chimney past small stances to a larger one in the chimney.
2 40 feet. Continue up until it is possible to move out onto the right wall. Traverse back left — Faith and Friction — to the main slab and

go up to a stance on the right. Or avoid the Faith and Friction slab by continuing straight up instead of moving right.

3 120 feet. Continue up easily until one can move right onto a large crevassed ledge.

4 90 feet. The Overhang. From the right hand end of the ledge climb the overhang strenuously on large but well spaced holds. Move up a little, then right and up a short chimney to easy ground.

Variation Finishes

The West Direct Finish 100 feet Hard Severe

4a 100 feet. From the stance traverse right round the arête and go up across the slab, then back left. Continue up the short chimney to easy ground.

The Direct Finish 80 feet Hard Very Severe *(1947)*

4b 80 feet. From the stance step left onto the continuation slab. Climb this and the loose chimney to the top. A very good pitch.

* **Ghecko Groove** 150 feet Extremely Severe (1959)

A delicate and sustained climb, interesting but poorly protected. The climb takes the narrow slab between Longland's and White Slab.

Start: Descend from the foot of Longland's to a small stance below the narrow slab.

1 80 feet. Climb into the groove from the left and continue up it to a protection peg under the overhang. Turn the overhang on the left and continue up to a belay, junction with White.

2 70 feet. Climb the groove to a protection peg at 30 feet. Traverse left to the arête and continue up to belay on Longland's. Finish up Longland's, The Direct Finish being appropriate.

Variation

2a 70 feet. Climb the groove for a few feet to a sloping ledge. Go left to the arête and climb straight up this.

*** **White Slab** 565 feet Mild Extremely Severe (1 pt. aid) (1956)

A tremendous route of great character with varied climbing and fine positions. One of the best climbs of its grade in Wales. It takes the obvious hourglass-shaped slab but starts further to the right.

Start: About 100 feet right of where the Eastern Terrace runs into the ground the overhangs are split by a wet grassy groove, that of Bow. Just to the right of this a small shattered rib leans against the overhangs.

1 60 feet. Step off the rib and make a difficult horizontal traverse left into a shallow groove. Continue left to the next wet groove. Up this to a large flake belay. Care should be taken to protect the second man on this pitch.

2 80 feet. Climb the groove and crack behind the stance, as for Bow, to belay just above the bottom of the White Slab itself.
3 120 feet. From the bottom of the slab go up a few feet then diagonally left to the arête — Linnell's Leap in reverse. Follow the arête, past a protection peg, to a spike at 60 feet. Step right and go up the thin crack to a flake. Go left round the edge and up a few feet to belay as for Ghecko.
4 65 feet. From the edge of the slab lasso a small spike on the opposite side and use the rope to cross the slab. Move up past the spike, traverse 10 feet left and go up to a good peg belay.
5 120 feet. Keeping near the edge of the slab, go up for 60 feet to a ledge. Continue up, past a protection peg, to a peg belay on the ledge.
6 30 feet. Traverse left and up to the crevassed stance of Longland's.
7 90 feet. Finish up Longland's although the Direct Finish, which takes the slab on the left, is more in keeping with the lower pitches.

Variations
2a 80 feet. Traverse diagonally left and up the groove round the corner. Harder than the normal way.
3a 100 feet. Climb the obvious diagonal crack to the arête. Climb the arête above the spike direct. Harder.
4a 65 feet. From the arête climb diagonally across to the small spike. Continue up to the peg belay.
4b 60 feet. From the edge of the slab climb the arête for 10 feet then climb steeply right across an incipient groove to the stance.
5a 140 feet. Traverse right from the peg runner into the groove (Walsh's Groove), climb this to the overhang and continue through the Cannon Hole to the crevassed stance. For slim climbers only.

*** **West Buttress Eliminate** 515 feet Extremely Severe (1962)
A superb route, one of the best on the West Buttress. Slightly flawed by its proximity to easier routes but the climbing on each individual pitch is excellent and independent, the highlight of the route being Walsh's Groove, a brilliant back and footing pitch high on the crag.
Start: Under the red groove directly below White Slab.
1 55 feet. Climb the red groove until holds lead right onto grass ledges. Up these to a large block belay.
2 70 feet. Climb the steep slabby groove on the left and move slightly left and up a short wall. Continue up to the right to spike belays at the foot of the White Slab.
3 120 feet. Climb the groove above and the diagonal crack to a flake belay on the right.
4 150 feet. Climb the short groove above. Climb the main groove to its top. Move left to belay as for White.
5 and **6** 120 feet. As for White Slab.

***Sheaf** 465 feet Very Severe (1945)

A fine, exposed and complex route weaving its way through the sheaf of ribs between the White and Narrow Slabs. Strenuous in its upper half.

1 and **2** 110 feet. As for Narrow Slab.

3 45 feet. From the stance beside White descend a few feet and swing round the corner to the right. Up grassy ledges to a stance and block belay.

4 40 feet. Up to a large corner stance above cracked blocks.

5 40 feet. Step out left and go up the steep slab to a small ledge on the arête. Move round the corner and go up to a broken chimney for a few feet to a poor stance and belays.

6 90 feet. Traverse left and slightly down onto the White Slab itself, and go up this a few feet then back right into a short groove. Up this for 10 feet to good runners then up for holds on the right arête. Swing out right and step into the groove on the right. Up this to a small ledge and belay in the groove above.

7 60 feet. Make a long stride to a good hold on the right. Pull round the corner onto Narrow Slab and up this to a stance.

8 80 feet. Easily up grass to a stance above the overhang on Longland's.

***Sheaf Direct** 415 feet Extremely Severe

A difficult and interesting climb.

Start: As for White Slab at the pinnacle.

1 150 feet. Start as for White Slab but go up immediately into a small clean cut groove. Continue directly for 60 feet to easy ground. Follow this to belay as for Sheaf.

2 85 feet. As for pitches 3 and 4 of Sheaf.

3 100 feet. Climb straight up the groove to a good resting place. Step left and climb a thin crack, then continue up the main groove to a sloping foothold. Use holds on the right arête to reach a large spike. Continue more easily to belay on Sheaf.

4 80 feet. Climb the groove for 20 feet, then go up a subsidiary groove in the right wall until it is possible to escape onto Narrow Slab, which is then followed to the top.

***Narrow Slab** 475 feet Very Severe (1933)

Takes the obvious narrow and uniform slab just left of the central mass of Bow and Great. The main pitches are hard but short. Linnell's Leap will probably be found as hard as anything above. The route begins by traversing in from the Eastern Terrace.

Start: At the bottom of this, just above the wet grass fall, at a grassy crack.

1 60 feet. Up the crack and its continuation to a small stance close under the rib of White Slab.

2 50 feet. Pull onto the sloping ledge on the right and step across onto White Slab. Step across and down a few feet — Linnell's Leap. Good flake belays a little higher.
3 45 feet. Descend a little and go right to ledges. Up and across to the foot of the Narrow Slab itself. Belay a little higher on the far side of the slab.
4 50 feet. Climb the thin crack in the slab to a slight bulge, then go diagonally left to the edge. Up to an awkward stance.
5 40 feet. Easily up for a few feet, then move right to the bottom of a flake. Up this to a small stance and belay.
6 40 feet. Climb the shallow groove in the slab, then a wider crack leads to a good stance.
7 and **8** 190 feet. Easily up grassy cracks with a stance at 100 feet. Continue to the top of the cliff. It is probably worth moving right onto Bow-Shaped Slab at the top of pitch 6 to save the grassy climbing.

The Arrow 300 feet Extremely Severe (1 pt. aid) (1964)
The second pitch is grassy and greasy.
Start: 30 feet left of Great Slab at a block leaning against the overhangs.
1 150 feet. Step off the block and climb up to a peg. Use this and continue leftwards to a ledge on the far arête. Climb the slab above, first left and then straight up to grass at 120 feet. Move left to the stance below Narrow.
2 150 feet. Climb the groove bounding the right hand side of Narrow Slab. Finish up the easy upper section of the slab, or up Bow.

Quiver 110 feet Extremely Severe (1974)
A very exposed and poorly protected pitch taking the left arête up the lower half of Bow-Shaped Slab to join that route after the traverse. Unfortunately it is a contrived line as all the holds lead up right away from the arête.
Start: As for Bow Right Hand at the cave stance of Great Slab.
1 110 feet. Climb to a ledge at 10 feet. Go straight up or layback up the flake from the right. Up to a horizontal fault and continue a few feet right of the arête to another fault. Move left to a ledge on the arête. Climb this to a belay by some loose blocks.

* **Bow-Shaped Slab** 625 feet Very Severe (1941)
A devious entry but fine upper pitches.
Start: At the bottom of the Eastern Terrace, as for Narrow. Scramble up to a grass ledge with an ash tree on the left.
1 25 feet. Climb across right to the corner and up this to large spikes.
2 90 feet. Traverse round the corner on the right and go up diagonally into a crack. Climb this and broken rocks to a stance beside

White Slab.

3 90 feet. Descend a little and swing round the corner to ledges. Cross these past Narrow Slab to the cave stance of Great Slab.

4 80 feet. Step round to the right and go up to a stance and belay.

5 120 feet. Go up a few feet and traverse left with one's feet on the obvious line. Continue up cracks to a stance and flake belay in the middle of the slab.

6 100 feet. Continue in the same line. Stance a few feet past the final skyline edge of the slab.

7 120 feet. Climb out of the recess on the left, then back right onto the rib. Up this.

*** **Great-Bow Combination** 550 feet Very Severe

A superb and very direct way up the cliff. Climb as for Great Slab to the cave stance at the top of the first pitch and then continue as for Bow-Shaped Slab.

** **Bow Right Hand** 320 feet Extremely Severe (1962)

A fine route in a very exposed position. The crux pitch builds up slowly in difficulty to a very hard move at 60 feet and then the climbing relents, with the third pitch in a tremendous position above the overhangs.

Start: At the cave stance on Great Slab.

1 80 feet. Climb the scoop to the stance at the start of the Bow traverse. Poorly protected.

2 120 feet. Climb up the blunt arête for 60 feet. Continue more easily to a shallow grassy groove and up this to a small stance and nut belay.

3 120 feet. Go straight up and traverse left to the lip of the overhangs. Follow these to the stance on Bow, which is then followed to the top.

Direct Start 120 feet Very Severe (1 pt. aid) (*1971*)

Start: 15 feet left of Great Slab.

1 120 feet. Pull over the overhang with a peg for aid and climb up leftwards to a small ledge. Continue up the shallow groove to the cave stance.

* **Great Slab** 580 feet Very Severe (1930)

A long and varied climb. The 40-foot corner can be very hard if wet, otherwise the first moves will be found as hard as anything. The upper pitches across the main slab are very exposed and feel serious.

Start: At an obvious break about 50 yards up the Western Terrace. A small rock pillar leans against the overhangs, below a short slab capped by an overhang and with a long groove on its left.

1 130 feet. Climb up and across the slab to reach the groove. Climb this to its top to a good ledge and cave belay.
2 130 feet. Go round the edge on the right and climb up for about 40 feet until one can traverse across to a shallow corner below a minor overhang. Go right and up easy ground to belay at the back of the 40-foot corner.
3 40 feet. Climb the corner. At 20 feet make a move left to gain the groove above. Up this to a good stance.
4 5 and **6** 280 feet. Continue up more easily in a diagonal line to the left across the main slab. Finish up the far edge to the top.

Variation
The Top Traverse 140 feet Very Severe (*1937*)
2a 80 feet. From the cave stance move right and climb straight up to a stance.
3a 60 feet. Continue up for 5 feet to a quartz ledge. Follow the obvious quartz-marked traverse across to the right to the foot of the 40-foot corner.

Syth 560 feet Extremely Severe (1 pt. aid) (1971)
A good and difficult route taking a direct line up the centre of Great Slab. The name is Welsh for "straight up".
Start: As for Great Slab.
1 100 feet. Climb to the overhang and over it at its right hand side. Up to below a second overhang and climb this with a sling for aid. Protection peg on the right of the slab above. Move up and left until it is possible to move right onto ledges below a groove. Peg belay.
2 120 feet. Climb the groove to reach the end of the traverse of Great. Reverse the traverse and go up to belay as for Bow.
3 130 feet. Climb up for 5 feet as for the Top Traverse. Continue half way along this then go straight up to some grass patches. Continue to belay in the middle of the slab (on Great Slab).
4 130 feet. Climb straight up with a protection peg at 35 feet to a peg belay at some shattered blocks. A poorly protected pitch.
5 80 feet. Moving slightly right climb up the middle of the slab to a grass traverse left. Follow this to the top.

***Moss Groove** 250 feet Hard Very Severe (1953)
Good climbing up the continuation of the 40-foot corner to the top of the cliff. Very hard in wet conditions.
Start: At the top of the 40-foot corner.
1 30 feet. From the top of the 40-foot corner traverse diagonally left, as for Great Slab, to a small terrace.
2 130 feet. A slightly rising traverse leads back into the corner where the crack narrows. Up and left for a few feet, then back into the corner. Up to a stance below the large overhangs. The groove can be climbed

direct from the top of the 40-foot corner but this is harder and needs 160 feet of rope.

3 90 feet. Turn the overhangs on the left by the wide crack and continue to the top.

Central Rib 300 feet Very Severe (1946)

A strenuous crack pitch, then easier climbing up the rib to the right of Moss Groove.

Start: At the foot of the 40-foot corner.

1 40 feet. Either climb the corner for 15 feet, step right and go up to the foot of the crack, or climb all the corner and descend to the foot of the crack.

2 90 feet. Climb the crack to a stance at 50 feet. Climb the groove on the left, pull out right and go across to a break in the rib. Step round and go up to a stance in the grass gully.

3 60 feet. Moderate climbing on the rib, keeping to the crest until it steepens.

4 110 feet. Continue up to the top.

***Mynedd** 540 feet Extremely Severe (1 pt. aid) (1966)

A fine route taking a complex line through slabs and overhangs to the left of Slanting. Unfortunately the climb starts with a somewhat dangerous prussik but once done, it adds character to the route. The prussik is the only aid used.

Start: About halfway up the Terrace between Great and Slanting at the widest point of the overhangs.

1 30 feet. Lasso a spike on the lip of the overhang and prussik up to it. Peg belay. Or lasso the peg.

2 120 feet. Cross the slab on the right and climb a short wall to the overhang. Jam out left to a protection peg and climb up left into a shallow groove on the arête. Climb the groove until forced left onto steeper rock. Traverse left to another weakness and follow this to an overhang. Step round left and cross a short wall to a grass rake. Follow this for 10 feet to a flake belay.

3 100 feet. Descend the rake for 5 feet and step onto the steep slab. Traverse right for 15 feet than climb up to the overhang. Move up left onto another slab and climb it for 20 feet to a stance..

4 150 feet. Climb the slab until it peters out. Move right to a rib and follow this to a ledge on the left. Climb a short wall to a downward pointing spike. Move right across overhanging rock to a spike on the arête. Continue past this descending slightly and cross Slanting Slab to another spike in a corner. Move right round the arête and climb a crack to a peg belay.

5 40 feet. A short slab and crack to a stance.

6 100 feet. Scramble to the top.

Spartacus 400 feet Mild Extremely Severe and A3 (1966)
A poor route with unpleasant pegging on doubtful pegs to surmount the overhang.
Start: 40 feet left of Slanting underneath a prominent crack.
1 130 feet. Climb a shattered wall to the roof. Peg out over this (5 pegs). Climb the crack above to a small overhang and go up the arête on the left for 30 feet to join Slanting. Follow Slanting left for 30 feet and then move right to a grass ledge and peg belay.
2 70 feet. Climb straight up to a shallow groove. Climb this and move right at the top to belay as for Gael.
3 and **4** 200 feet. As for Gael.

** **Slanting Slab** 450 feet Mild Extremely Severe (3 pts. aid) (1955)
An excellent route giving reasonable climbing in a very exposed position.
Start: From a pinnacle under the overhangs below the start of Bloody Slab.
1 120 feet. Using 3 pegs and slings move left round the overhang onto the slab. Traverse almost horizontally left past a grass patch to a grass rake. Go up this to a stance and spike belay in the corner.
2 40 feet. Continue up the rake and step round the corner to a large slab. Nut belays a short way up the flake crack in this.
3 140 feet. Climb the slab to a large overhang. Step left and go up a narrow white slab to another overhang. Traverse right and pull over the overhang to the groove above. Up this or the right arête to belay.
4 150 feet. Scramble up the gully to the top.

Gael 380 feet Extremely Severe (3 pts. aid) (1962)
Climbs the overhang and slab above the traverse of Slanting.
1 110 feet. Climb the overhang with three points of aid, as for Slanting. Traverse left past a grass patch to a second grass patch. Climb the overhang via a thin crack on the left and go up the slab above. Move right into the crack and climb this to a grass rake. Stance at the top of this but no belay. Or nut belay a few feet lower but no stance.
2 70 feet. Climb the rib above to the overhangs. Step left and down into a groove, and traverse diagonally left to grass ledges on the left of the overhangs. Peg belay.
3 100 feet. Climb the wall above, step left to a groove and go up this to a grass ramp.
4 100 feet. Scrambling to the top.

***Fibrin** 340 feet Mild Extremely Severe (4 pts. aid) (1966)
A link pitch joining the start of Slanting with the large grass field below and to the left of Bloody.
1 80 feet. Over the overhang as for Slanting (3 pts. of aid). Move left to a grass patch. Peg and nut belay.

2 140 feet. Climb up to the overhang and move right on undercuts across the foot of a groove to a peg on the slab. Use this and climb the slab for 20 feet to a poor spike (protection peg) and swing right to another groove. Follow this to a crack below a slab and overhang. Left for a few feet up the slab then right below the overhang. Climb this using good holds on the right then move left to grass ledges and peg belays.
3 120 feet. Follow the rib above to join the easy upper section of Bloody.

Thrombin 300 feet Mild Extremely Severe (1966)
A good pitch but a bit loose and unprotected. It takes the thin crack in the large slab on the left of Bloody Slab.
Start: Lower down the terrace than for Bloody, at a big spike belay.
1 150 feet. Step left and climb the groove to a large sloping hold. Protection peg. Traverse left into the thin crack and climb this for 50 feet to a good resting place. Protection peg. Continue up to a grass sod, step right then traverse horizontally left to the large grass ledges below pitch 2 of Bloody.
2 and **3** 150 feet. Finish up Bloody (part of pitch 2 and pitch 3).

** **Bloody Slab** 300 feet Extremely Severe (1952)
A tremendous route giving delicate slab climbing, which takes a diagonal line up the right hand side of the obvious big red slab.
Start: At a large flake at the bottom right hand side of the slab where the overhangs peter out.
1 100 feet. Climb diagonally left for 30 feet to a small flake runner. Climb straight up over the bulge and go up the flake crack to the triangular overhang. Turn this on the left and go up to a small sloping stance and peg belay.
2 90 feet. Traverse left and go up to a small ledge. Continue left to grass and go up the grass gully on the left.
3 110 feet. Climb the rib on the left to the top.

Variations
1a 110 feet. Hard Very Severe. This avoids the main difficulty of the climb. Climb diagonally left for 30 feet to a small flake runner. Step left and down onto the loose finger of rock. Climb straight up the small bow-shaped slab to the stance.
2a 90 feet. Follow Syncope up the crack to the roof, then traverse left under this to the belay on the normal line.

Syncope 300 feet Extremely Severe (2 pts. aid) (1971)
A direct finish to Bloody Slab taking the large overhangs above with aid.
1 100 feet. As for Bloody Slab.

2 140 feet. Climb left and up to a small ledge as for Bloody. Move left again to a crack in the slab. Climb this to the roof. Climb up into a groove in the roof, on the right. Use a peg and a nut to gain the slab above. Go left and up to a small ledge then climb up right to a corner, and a ledge above. Peg belays.
3 60 feet. Left onto the slab and up to its top. Scrambling remains .

** **Haemogoblin** 300 feet Mild Extremely Severe (1962)
An excellent, interesting and well protected climb taking the obvious groove to the right of Bloody Slab. Often wet.
Start: As for Bloody.
1 90 feet. Climb the groove past two protection pegs to a sloping stance and peg belays.
2 90 feet. Climb the groove for 30 feet to a chockstone. Traverse left across the slab to a crack. Climb this and the overhanging crack to a stance and belay.
3 120 feet. Easily up to the top.

Carpet Slab 250 feet Very Severe (1953)
Hard for its grade for about 40 feet but easy and grassy after that. Climbs the obvious vegetated slab to the right of Bloody.
Start: Below the centre of the slab.
1 120 feet. Go strenuously up to the thin crack. Climb this and the slab above.
2 130 feet. Climb to the top via as much rock as possible.

Diwedd Groove 290 feet Extremely Severe (2 pts. aid) (1965)
A difficult route with some thin groove climbing and a hard overhang.
Start: As for Carpet Slab.
1 80 feet. Follow Carpet Slab until a traverse right can be made just below the small overlap. Peg belay in the groove.
2 150 feet. Climb the groove and move left round the first overhang. Use a peg for aid to gain a crack on the right of the second overhang and climb this to a chockstone on the lip of the overhang. Using a sling on this move out onto the right wall. Traverse round the corner to a stance and belay below another overhang.
3 60 feet. Traverse right under the overhang to the edge of the slab. Up this to the top.

Variation
Direct Start 80 feet Aid
This was the original start and uses several nuts for aid.
Start: To the right of Carpet, below some shattered cracks in the overhangs.
1a 80 feet. Climb the crack with several nuts for aid. Climb the slab above then move left into the groove proper to the stance.

The Leastest 170 feet Very Severe (2 pts. aid) (1961)
A poor and rather pointless route.
Start: To the right of Carpet Slab where the Terrace almost meets the overhangs.
1 50 feet. Move up over shattered spikes and swing left to a shallow scoop using 2 pegs for aid. Climb up leftwards over loose flakes to a narrow ledge and a groove. Up this to a grass ledge.
2 60 feet. Easily left to the edge and up to a stance and belay below the obvious overhang.
3 60 feet. Turn the overhang on the right and follow the ridge to the top.

*__The West Buttress Girdle__ 985 feet Hard Very Severe (1949)
A long expedition, sustained at a good standard, and strenuous. It follows the whole of Sheaf and then links the cruces of the old West Buttress routes, finishing by a long diagonal traverse above Slanting and Bloody Slabs.
Start: At the foot of Longland's proper.
1 35 feet. Descend to the right to a stance in the corner, close under the rib of White Slab.
2 50 feet. Pull up onto a ledge on the right and step round the rib on to the White Slab itself. Move across and down a little to grass. This is Linnell's Leap.
3 45 feet. This and the next four pitches are as for Sheaf. Descend a little and swing round the corner to grass ledges. Up to a good stance and block belay.
4 40 feet. Continue up to a large corner stance above some cracked blocks.
5 40 feet. Step out to the left and go up the steep slab making for the ledge on the edge. Move round the corner into a broken chimney and go up it a few feet to a poor stance and belays.
6 90 feet. Traverse left and down slightly onto White Slab. Up a little and back right into a small groove. Up this awkwardly to good belays but no stance. Make a bold swing out to the right, on good holds, and continue up the layback crack on the right to a small terrace.
7 70 feet. Make a long stride to the right and round onto the upper reaches of Narrow Slab. Ascend for a few feet to a running belay, then descend easily to a stance and belay in the grassy crack.
8 40 feet. Descend a few feet from the stance and step across onto a subsidiary rib on the right. Cross the groove and go out to a grass ledge breaking onto Bow-Shaped Slab. Climb up to a stance and belay 15 feet higher.
9 85 feet. Descend again to a grass ledge at the end of the Bow traverse. Reverse this, keeping one's feet in the obvious diagonal break. This leads to a stance at the far end. Climb up to a small stance

a little higher to bring the second man across.
10 60 feet. Traverse horizontally across on the quartz-marked line. This gets more difficult towards the end and leads to the grass field below the 40-foot corner. This is the Top Traverse of Great Slab.
11 40 feet. Climb the slabby corner to a good stance.
12 90 feet. Descend to the foot of the Central Rib crack on the right, and go up this to a break in the rib.
13 50 feet. Scramble easily along the grassy rake across the shallow gully to a stance on the skyline.
14 60 feet. Continue in the same line on good holds and grass.
15 60 feet. The line becomes more serious again. Away on the right is a quartz break above the overhangs of Bloody Slab. Traverse across, descending slightly, then make an awkward pull into a grassy groove. Step round to a stance just above the overhang.
16 90 feet. Keep in the same line, rather higher than before; at 35 feet is a hand traverse leading to more grass. Then a delicate toe traverse across a slab, with a step-up at the end to a small bilberry ledge. Step round into the deep grassy chimney on the right.
17 40 feet. Easily up the chimney to finish on the ridge.

** **New Girdle** 1500 feet Extremely Severe (6 pts. aid) (1966)
A very long and difficult expedition with some excellent climbing and a short artificial pitch.
Start: As for The Boulder.
1 2 and **3** 225 feet. As for The Boulder until it is possible to move right across the wall and down a groove to Longland's.
4 80 feet. Descend Longland's to Ghecko Groove.
5 70 feet. Abseil down Ghecko to the stance common with White.
6 65 feet. From the arête on the right climb diagonally across the slab to a small spike. Move up, back left and up again to belay.
7 to **11** 345 feet. Follow the Old Girdle (pitches 6 to 10) to the 40-foot corner on Great Slab.
12 100 feet. Descend the grass ledges then traverse right across a small slab to a corner. Down 10 feet to a belay, common with Mynedd.
13 80 feet. The Link. Climb down a few feet and step onto the steep slab on the right. Climb up towards the overhang until it is possible to traverse to a flake in the middle of the slab. Continue by a difficult ascending traverse to join Slanting at a grass ledge. Descend Slanting to a belay.
14 50 feet. Continue the descent of Slanting and reverse its traverse to a grass ledge.
15 140 feet. Climb up to the overhang and move right under the groove. Climb onto the next slab with a peg for aid. Climb up for 20 feet to a spike on the right overlap. Swing across onto a small ledge and crack. Follow the crack and groove above onto a small slab on the left. Traverse the slab and go up to an overhang. Climb this on the

right on good holds and go left to grass ledges and peg belay (Fibrin pitch 2).
16 40 feet. Move right and reverse the top traverse of Bloody Slab to a peg belay in the corner.
17 25 feet. Descend slightly and go round the corner on the right to a slab. Go right to a bulge and ascend this on flat holds to the belay on Haemogoblin.
18 60 feet. Move right and climb the overhanging wall with 5 pegs for aid. Pull onto grass ledges and then follow a grassy crack to a belay on a large spike.
19 70 feet. Descend the grass for 20 feet then traverse across a slab into Diwedd Groove. Descend this to a belay.
20 150 feet. Climb out of Diwedd Groove onto the next overlap then descend grooves until under an overhang and on a weakness leading right. Follow this over a small overhang then go right again to a groove. Follow the groove to grass ledges. Go right to the end of the cliff. A very loose pitch.

The Steep Band

Below the Western Terrace is a steep band of smooth rock. This is split at three quarters height by a rock terrace, parallel to the Western Terrace, and called the Giant's Trod. In the lower part of the band is a steep slab running into a large overhanging amphitheatre. For climbs finishing on the Giant's Trod it is advisable to continue up this and descend the Western Terrace. None of the routes are particularly worthwhile.

Metamorphosis 140 feet Very Severe (1974)
Start: To the left of Beano at a black looking crack, often wet.
1 140 feet. Climb the crack to the terrace and continue on to the top.

Beano 120 feet Extremely Severe (1 pt. aid) (1975)
A difficult climb taking thin cracks to the left of the central amphitheatre.
Start: At the second crack left of Steep Band.
1 120 feet. Climb up for 15 feet and use a high peg for aid, then climb the crack above. Step left into a shallow chimney and climb this moving left at the top to a small pinnacle. Climb up to thin cracks and traverse right to a thin flake crack. Climb this and the grooves above to easier ground. Continue to a peg belay on the terrace.

Steep Band 110 feet Very Severe (1960)
A pleasant route but not really worthwhile except as a short route with which to end the day. The route traverses across the slab below the overhanging amphitheatre and finishes up the two obvious grooves on the left.
Start: Scramble up the right hand side of the slab until level with the bottom of the right hand of the two grooves.
1 30 feet. Cross the slab at a low level to the bottom of the groove.
2 80 feet. Climb the groove for 15 feet. Move left into the other groove. Climb this to the Giant's Trod.

Apollo 160 feet Mild Extremely Severe and A1 (1970)
Takes the overhanging groove on the right of Steep Band.
Start: At the bottom of the slab, right of Steep Band.
1 50 feet. Climb the middle of the slab to a niche under the roofs. Peg belay but no stance.
2 110 feet. Go round the overhang using a nut and a peg for aid. Climb the groove to the second overhang and go over this using a peg for aid. The groove above using a peg and a nut for aid shortly before

the top.

***Head for Heights** 200 feet Extremely Severe (4 pts.aid) (1975)
A strenuous and technical route which breaks through the overhangs to the right of Apollo.
Start: Right of Apollo, at the arête.
1 80 feet. Start from the arête and climb diagonally left up a small slab below the roof, past a protection peg. Use a higher peg and swing round the corner, then move left using a high nut. Use another nut to to exit from the overhangs and climb a short crack to a stance and peg belay.
2 120 feet. Use combined tactics to leave the stance moving leftwards. Climb up past a loose flake. Traverse right a few feet and climb the groove above to the top.

The Far West Buttress

Down and to the right of the Steep Band is the large buttress of the Far West. Viewed face on it is shaped like a broad diamond, about 500 feet high in the middle. There are three distinct lines on the buttress, Slanting Chimney on the left, Deep Chimney in the centre and Forgotten Gully on the right. All three lines slant up from left to right.

This Buttress gives several climbs up to Very Severe, most of them starting around or to the left of the toe of the buttress. Moving right from Deep Chimney there is a very steep wall before the next route, Forgotten Gully. Further right again is a huge recessed section of cliff with a steep back wall. Sun Dance takes a crack in this. Further right the rock becomes of poorer quality but beyond the Far West, across scree are some smaller slabs about 150 feet high with some interesting problems.

As the whole buttress lacks obvious feature between the major lines, route finding can be very demanding and one can easily get lost among the numerous small ribs and slabs.

The most obvious way down from the routes is down the Far Western Terrace, parallel to the Western Terrace but this is NOT recommended due to very poor rock. Instead the best method is to scramble up right to the top of the buttress and walk westwards down the ridge scree-slope to a flat grassy area well to the west of the main crag. From here an easy open gully provides a safe and fast descent. At the foot of the gully the path continues down diagonally to the foot of the crag. Alternatively go up the ridge to the Western Terrace and down this.

* **Slanting Chimney** 250 feet Severe (1919)
A good climb which can be quite hard in adverse conditions.
Start: At the foot of the chimney, which is the obvious line on the left hand side of the buttress.
1 40 feet. Up easily, and follow the crack to a ledge and belay.
2 90 feet. Climb up into the chimney and follow it strenuously to a large grass ledge and belay.
3 120 feet. Continue up the chimney to finish just left of a huge jammed block. Or climb the clean rib on the left of the chimney.

Variation
The Original Finish
3a 65 feet. Climb the chimney for 20 feet and step out right to a

ramp leading up right (Care should be taken as there is another line leading out right lower). Move up right and ascend steeply up a rib to a ledge below a small overhang.

4a 95 feet. Traverse right along the ledge, then follow first a groove, then a rib, making for a deep groove on the right. Climb this to a grassy recess then easily up to finish.

Wapentake 360 feet Very Severe (1973)
Twenty feet right of Slanting Chimney, and parallel to it, is a crack, grassy in its lower section.
Start: Where the crack meets the scree.
1 85 feet. Follow the crack on either side to a grass ledge.
2 45 feet. Make a move up the crack then pull out right onto a ledge. Move 5 feet right, up a crack then back left to the main crack. Up to a grassy ledge.
3 100 feet. Easily up right for 20 feet to a shallow scoop split by a thin crack. Up this to a grass ledge. Move left onto the wall and gain an obvious hold. Up left to a spike and take the groove above to a large field below a corner. Spike belay.
4 80 feet. Up the slab on the left and up a short rib to a ledge below an overhang. Move right and turn the overhang by an obvious crack. Climb the groove to a small terrace below small overhangs.
5 50 feet. Easy rock leads to broken ground. Scramble to the top.

Primitive Route 380 feet Very Difficult (1919)
A good mountaineering route.
Start: At a ledge just left of the foot of the buttress, below a short corner.
1 90 feet. Climb the corner or a harder crack on the right, to a prominent jammed block. Move right a few feet and climb the left-ward slanting crack near the left edge of the slabs. Good stance and belay.
2 50 feet. Up broken rock to a huge grassy bay below the twin chimneys.
3 80 feet. Climb the right hand chimney for 30 feet. Step left and continue up the left hand chimney. Up diagonally right to a good stance and peg belay.
4 25 feet. Up right to an obvious stance and flake belay.
5 25 feet. Climb the small corner and the short slab to grass and another belay.
6 80 feet. Traverse up left across ledges to a short corner. Or climb the corner above the belay to overhanging rock. Traverse 50 feet left, past a chimney at half way, to belay on a grassy ledge below the corner. Better.
7 30 feet. Climb the corner to a grassy recess.

Variation
The Direct Finish 120 feet Very Severe
Start: At the top of pitch 5.
6a 120 feet. Climb a small rib on the right of the stance passing a large grass ledge on the right. After another 20 feet gain a smaller ledge below a flake crack. Climb this to where it widens and continue up to small ledges. Easily up the corner for a few feet then step right to the arête and climb this.

Slab Climb-Left Hand 550 feet Severe (1919)
Start: Just left of the toe of the buttress.
1 75 feet. Climb up leftwards on sloping sills of rock to a small ledge. Just right of starting ledge of Primitive Route. Climb the cracked wall above for 10 feet, then move right on to the slab and climb this diagonally right for 20 feet, then climb straight up to the furrow. Belay below an obvious crack.
2 100 feet. Climb the crack and continue up grass ledges to the left end of a large field.
3 70 feet. Climb the indefinite crack to a large flake. From the top of this move right up the slab to a ledge. It is now best to descend diagonally left down the break to belay.
4 95 feet. Easily back right rising slightly along the grassy break to join Slab Climb-Right Hand and continue to belay in Deep Chimney.
5 and **6** 210 feet. As for Slab Climb-Right Hand pitches 4 and 5.

****Slab Climb-Right Hand** 550 feet Hard Severe (1919)
A delightful route on excellent slabs.
Start: Just left of the toe of the buttress.
1 120 feet. Traverse right for 20 feet on the sloping sills of rock to a corner. Climb this and at the top climb diagonally right up the pleasant slab. Belay on the blunt spike at the top of the grass furrow.
2 80 feet. Easily up grass on the left until it is possible to step up right to the foot of the large slab. Easily up to a ledge and peg belay.
3 140 feet. Move diagonally right to the edge of the slab and follow the edge past ledges at 100 feet and 120 feet to belay at 140 feet in Deep Chimney.
4 140 feet. Move left onto the slab and take the most pleasant looking line to easier rock.
5 70 feet. Easily up an obvious arête on the right. 150 feet of easy scrambling remain.

Parapet Route 235 feet Severe
An artificial and devious route.
1 75 feet. As for Slab Climb-Left Hand.
2 40 feet. Take the slab above or a shallow groove to a narrow rake. Follow this to Deep Chimney and step across to a rock recess.

3 120 feet. Traverse a few feet right then descend to the lip of the overhang. Work obliquely up right for 70 feet, keeping to the edge. The slab finishes in a grassy recess. 250 feet of scrambling remains.

Deep Chimney 370 feet Very Difficult (1905)
A good climb.
Start: In the corner below the chimney at the foot of the crack.
1 60 feet. Climb a few feet up the crack then traverse left on good holds to the corner. Round the corner to a grassy stance. Make a delicate step up above the stance. After a few feet follow broken ledges to a stance beside the deep chimney.
2 80 feet. Step into the chimney and climb it to an uncomfortable stance but good belay at 80 feet.
3 4 and **5** 230 feet. Continue up the bed of the chimney to the top. Stances at 50 and 100 feet.

Variation
Direct Start 90 feet Severe
Directly below the line of Deep Chimney is a right-angled groove. Climb this to a stance at the foot of the chimney. A pleasant pitch.

Round past the steep wall is Forgotten Gully, which is taken by the next two climbs. The logical line to take is Sea of Cloud to the peg runner on pitch 2 and continue up Road of Ghosts.

Sea of Cloud 470 feet Very Severe (1972)
The climb starts up Forgotten Gully, then escapes left to reach the upper slabs.
1 75 feet. Climb the gully until a move can be made out left to a slab (just below the pasture). Right up the slab until a move can be made right round an arête onto grass. Up the corner to a ledge.
2 95 feet. Climb the corner crack past a protection peg at 40 feet. Above the peg take the obvious groove above and to the left to a stance and belay.
3 4 and **5** 300 feet. Follow either easy slabs left of the gully, or the gully itself to the top.

Road of Ghosts 475 feet Very Severe (1972)
Takes the slabs on the right of Forgotten Gully, then climbs the gully direct.
Start: A few feet right of Forgotten Gully.
1 95 feet. Climb to an obvious flake which slants up right and follow this until a large grass ledge can be gained. Take a shallow groove on the left for 15 feet and traverse left to a ledge and peg belay.
2 120 feet. Step out right onto the slab and climb into the small corner above. Climb the crack, move left and up until a step left can

be made to join Sea of Cloud. Climb the corner past the peg runner and continue straight up the gully.
3 and **4** 260 feet. Easily up the gully or slabs on the left.

Sun Dance 480 feet Very Severe (1972)
Start: At the foot of the right hand corner of the huge recessed section of cliff right of Forgotten Gully.
1 120 feet. Traverse left across grass slabs for 90 feet to the base of a blunt arête, which is below and to the left of the obvious slanting crack. Traverse diagonally right to the foot of the crack. Nut belay.
2 120 feet. Climb the leftward slanting crack in the steep wall until a short groove leads to a large flake. Belay on top.
3 120 feet. Traverse left for 10 feet. Up a few feet until it is possible to move back right above the belay. Take the easiest line up slabs to a large belay.
4 120 feet. Easily up slabs to the top.

White Rose Garland 1,040 feet Hard Severe (1973)
A girdle traverse of the Far West. A not too serious mountaineering expedition, which requires either a knowledge of the other routes or natural route finding ability. The route is rather vegetated but contains some good pitches.
Start: In a corner about 70 feet below the Far Western Terrace.
1 145 feet. Follow the obvious traverse which goes across the buttress at half height to belay in Slanting Chimney.
2 45 feet. Up Slanting Chimney a few feet and climb a ramp on the right to a large grass ledge. Spike belay as for Wapentake.
3 90 feet. Move down right and round the arête. Traverse right for a few feet and make a step down to a grass ledge. Diagonally right up ledges to belay as for Primitive Route.
4 25 feet. Descend the short slab and corner. Pitch 5 of Primitive Route in reverse.
5 135 feet. On the right is an obvious grassy break leading to Deep Chimney. The pitch takes the rising traverse line 25 feet lower, on the clean slab. Step right and down 10 feet to reach the traverse line. Follow it to Deep Chimney. Up this for 30 feet to a spike belay.
6 110 feet. Move down 10 feet and wander right along the terrace until one can descend diagonally right down gardened rock to a corner at the top of a field.
7 160 feet. (can be split). Down the field until it is possible to move right round an arête. Up right into the corner. Climb up 10 feet to a good spike and continue up slabs for 45 feet until one can traverse right into Forgotten Gully.
8 25 feet. Up the gully for 10 feet, then out right to a flake belay.
9 75 feet. Move left 10 feet, then up a few feet and back left above the belay. Climb slabs to a belay.

10 75 feet. Go diagonally right down the pasture, making for a huge spike below the skyline rib. Belay at a huge flake below.
11 75 feet. From the flake, climb the rib for 15 feet until one can move right onto easy ledges. Follow the rightward slanting rake to a belay near a flake on the rake.
12 80 feet. Easily right and climb a grassy gully to finish.

Winter Climbing

The best winter climbing is to be found on the huge broken buttress on the left of the main cliffs, Garn Goch. It has several good icefalls in winter, the best of these being at about half height on the left. The steeper section of rock in the centre has routes on its left, right and centre, all at about Grade III.

A shallow gully about 200 yards left of the Far Far East holds snow well and is about II/III.

The various gullies on the main cliffs can provide pleasant snow climbs in impressive surroundings, the most notable being the gully just left of the Far Far East, the East Gully (finish up ledges on the left, not up the rocks), and the Eastern and Western Terraces. This last is very impressive under heavy snow conditions. The Eastern Terrace has a direct start, which takes a steep ice wall below Longland's, Grade III.

Several of the rock climbs have been done in winter but generally these remain rock routes with snow rather than true winter climbs. The exception is the Black Cleft which, in exceptional winters, gives a pyramid of steep ice, grade V.

First Ascents

1905	**Deep Chimney**	P S Thompson
1905 September	**East Wall Climb**	A P Abraham G D Abraham
1912 May	**East Gully**	G H L Mallory R Todhunter
1919	**Primitive Route** **Slab Climb** **Slanting Chimney** *The original Slab Climb probably took the easiest line up the rock now taken by Left Hand and Right Hand Slab Climbs.*	H R C Carr G A Lister
1927	**Pigott's Climb**	A S Pigott M Wood L Henshaw J F Burton
	The original climb did not climb the corners direct. The top crack was climbed in 1934 by J D Hoyland. The Wall Finish was climbed by R A Hodgkin. A D M Cox, Clare Mallory and Beridge Mallory on 23 June 1937. *The first pitch of* **Wall Variations** *was climbed by H I Banner and A T Griffith in 1957; the second pitch was climbed by H I Banner and B Ingle on 13 May 1961.*	
1928 Whitsun	**Longland's Climb**	J L Longland A S Pigott F S Smythe W Eversden M Wood
	The Direct Finish was added by J M Edwards and M P Wood in 1947	
1930 June 15	**Great Slab**	C F Kirkus G G Macphee
	The Green Caterpillar, once a prominent feature, has now disappeared. The Top Traverse was taken by R A Hodgkin, A D M Cox, Clare Mallory, and Beridge Mallory on June 21 1937.	
1931 August 3	**Chimney Route**	C F Kirkus J M Edwards
	At the time considered more difficult than Great Slab. Originally took the Rickety Innards finish. The	

	Crooked Finish was led by H E Kretschmer. The Continuation Chimney was led in August 1930 by C F Kirkus with G G Macphee.	
1931 August 30	**Pedestal Crack**	C F Kirkus G G Macphee
	Originally started up the rib on the right. The Direct Start was added on 15 June 1932 by C F Kirkus and M Linnell.	
1931	**Terrace Crack**	C F Kirkus and party
1931 October 25	**Bridge Groove**	C F Kirkus A W Bridge
1932 June 19	**Birthday Crack**	C F Kirkus M Linnell M Pallis
	It was the birthday of both Kirkus and Linnell.	
1932 June 19	**Curving Crack**	C F Kirkus A W Bridge M Linnell A B Hargreaves W S Dyson
	The party failed on the Direct Start, while Linnell soloed the first pitch. The Direct Start was added on 6 July 1940 by N P Piercy and A J Woodroffe.	
1932 June 26	**Direct Finish to the East Buttress**	C F Kirkus M Wood A S Pigott A W Bridge
1933	**Brwynog Chimney**	M S Taylor J R Jenkins
	Originally called Terrace Chimney.	
1933 August 18	**Narrow Slab**	M Linnell A S Pigott E Holliday P L Roberts
	The first ascent avoided the first section of slab by a groove on the left. The slab direct was probably first done by Kirkus.	
1935 May 5	**Jubilee Climb**	M S Taylor J R Jenkins T U L S O'Connor
1937 June 24	**Sunset Crack**	A D M Cox R A Hodgkin Clare Mallory Beridge Mallory
1941 September 20	**Bow-Shaped Slab**	J M Edwards J Cooper

		G F Parkinson

The modern way of doing the traverse was discovered by G Dwyer and J B Lawton in May 1948.

1945 October 17	**Sheaf**	J Campbell A D M Cox

A fine piece of route finding. The various pitches of **Sheaf Direct** *were climbed as follows: Top pitch by D D Whillans in 1959, pitch 3 by P Crew and D J S Cook on 31 May 1966, pitch 1 by A Rouse and J Cardy in June 1971.*

1946 May	**Central Rib**	G G Macphee H A Carsten
1949 May 21	**The West Buttress Girdle**	P R J Harding G Dyke
1951 June 24	**Diglyph**	J Brown M T Sorrell
1951 October 13	**Vember**	J Brown D D Whillans

A long standing problem. The first pitch was originally known as the Drainpipe Crack. Kirkus got some way up it in 1931 and it was led in 1937 by A Birtwistle.

1951 October 28	**The Boulder**	J Brown

The rest of the party was unable to follow and the upper part was climbed in one run out.
The variation finish was done by R James, A Ovchinnikov and J Walmsley on May 29 1960.

1952 May 4	**The Black Cleft**	J Brown D D Whillans *(Alternate leads)*

The Direct Start was added by E Metcalfe and B Fuller in 1959.

1952 June 6	**Pinnacle Flake**	J Brown D D Whillans *(Alternate leads)*

The Direct Finish was added by D D Whillans in 1957.

1952 June 7	**Spillikin**	J Brown D D Whillans *(Alternate leads)*
1952 June 10	**Bloody Slab**	J Streetly

The rest of the party were unable to follow. This was only Streetly's second climb on Cloggy. The alternative to the first pitch was found by P Walsh in 1959.

1952 June 14	**Llithrig**	J Brown J R Allen

1952 June 15	**Octo**	J Brown M T Sorrell D Belshaw
1952 June 20	**The Corner**	J Brown J R Allen D Belshaw
1953 March 14	**Moss Groove**	R Moseley L Rogerson
1953 May 9	**Gargoyle**	J Brown P G White
	The Direct Start was climbed by R Evans and J Pasquill on 17 July 1971.	
1953 May 10	**The East Buttress Girdle**	J Brown J R Allen D D Whillans
1953 June 7	**East Gully Wall**	J Brown D D Whillans
	Moseley's Variation was climbed by R Moseley, P G White and T Waghorn on 16 April 1954. The Direct Start was climbed by R Edwards and R Rejous on 9 May 1966.	
1953 June 14	**East Gully Groove**	D D Whillans J R Allen
	The Direct Start was climbed by J Smith and J Brown in 1957.	
1953 October 4	**Carpet Slab**	J Brown D D Whillans
1954 April 17	**Left Edge**	R Moseley
	The rest of the party were unable to follow. The modern way of doing it was found by D Whillans on the second ascent.	
1955 June 5	**Camus**	G J Sutton Miss C A Clarke
	Most of this had been done by the Abraham brothers in 1905.	
1955 July 9	**Slanting Slab**	D D Whillans V Betts
1955 August 30	**Woubits**	J Brown D D Whillans *(Alternate leads)*
1956 March	**The Sceptre**	J Brown D D Whillans
1956 April 1	**The Orb**	R Moseley J Smith
1956 April 19	**White Slab**	R Moseley J Smith

A long standing problem. The entry and the slab above Linnell's Leap had been previously climbed by J Brown, D T Roscoe, J R Allen and R Moseley. Moseley entered by Linnell's Leap to complete the ascent. The whole climb was done the next day by D D Whillans and D T Roscoe.
H I Banner climbed the variation to the 3rd pitch and went through the Cannon Hole in 1959.
J A Austin did the arête variation to the lasso pitch in 1959. J H Deacon found the modern way of finishing pitch 5; previously the pitch had traversed into Walsh's Groove.

1956 July 24	**Taurus**	D D Whillans J Brown
1957 March 30	**Moonshine**	H I Banner Miss D N Morin
	The Direct Finish was climbed by R Edwards and J Costello on August 20 1966.	
1957 April 9	**The Mostest**	J Brown
	The second was unable to follow. *The Direct Start was climbed by J Brown and J Smith in 1957.*	
1957 May 3	**November**	J Brown J Smith
	R Moseley had previously abseiled down and inserted about eight chockstones, which Brown used for aid. The first free ascent was made by A McHardy in 1970.	
1958 May 4	**Beanlands**	C T Jones B D Wright A Cowburn
1958 October 25	**Shrike**	J Brown H Smith J Smith
1959 May 17	**Ghecko Groove**	H I Banner R Beesley
	The variation finish was climbed by J A and Mrs Austin in 1962.	
1959 May 24	**Boomerang**	J Brown G D Verity
1959 September	**Woubits Left Hand**	J Brown M A Boysen
	The top corner originally used three points of aid. The first free ascent was made by A Sharp on June 30 1975.	

1959 October 4	**Troach**	H I Banner R G Wilson
1960 May 7	**The Hand Traverse**	H I Banner C T Jones
1960 May 28	**The Bauble**	C J Mortlock T Wiseman
1960 June 26	**Guinivere**	C T Jones M P Hatton
1960 October	**Steep Band**	C T Jones L Brown *(Alternate leads)*
	B Ingle led the second pitch free on the 2nd ascent.	
1961 May 22	**The Leastest**	L Noble C J Mortlock *(Alternate leads)*
1961 May 27	**Scorpio**	N J Soper P Crew
1961 August 31 / September 1-2	**The Pinnacle Girdle**	N J Soper P Crew *(Varied leads)*
	A long standing problem. The original finish went down East Gully Groove and up East Gully Wall variation finish. The modern finish was added by the same party on April 29 1962.	
1961 October 7	**Serth**	B Ingle P Crew *(Alternative leads)*
1962 April 27	**The Shadow**	P Crew B Ingle *(Varied leads)*
1962 April 28	**Daurigol**	B Ingle M A Boysen *(Alternate leads)*
	The second pitch originally used several points of aid. The first free ascent was made by R Evans, J Pasquill and J Syrett.	
1962 April 29	**Bow Right Hand**	N J Soper P Crew
	The final pitch had been climbed previously by N J Soper and P E Brown. The Direct Start was climbed by L E Holliwell and B Whybrow 19 August 1971.	
1962 May 2	**Haemogoblin**	B Ingle P Crew *(Varied leads)*
1962 May 27	**Great Wall**	P Crew
	It rained and the second did not follow. J Brown had	

	previously climbed what is now the first pitch. On the first ascent about eight points of aid were used. The first free ascent was made by J Allen on 28 June 1975. *The Arête Finish was climbed by A G Cramm and P Scott on May 29 1966.*	
1962 June 2	**Naddyn Ddu**	P Crew B Ingle *(Varied leads)*
	The Direct Start was climbed by A Strapcans on 17 May 1975.	
1962 June 3	**West Buttress Eliminate**	B Ingle P Crew *(Alternate leads)*
	The final groove was climbed by P Walsh in 1959 in mistake for Sheaf!	
1962 June 10	**Gael**	B C Webb B L Griffiths
1962 June 17	**Pinnacle Arête**	M Boysen C J Mortlock
1962 July 28	**The Croak**	D Yates R Phillips
1963 May	**Slurp**	C J Mortlock and party
1963 May	**Little Krapper**	C J Mortlock L Noble *(Varied leads)*
1963 September 21	**The Boldest**	P Crew B Ingle
	An expansion bolt was placed for protection; this was removed in 1973. The Direct Finish was climbed by C Phillips and P Minks in 1969.	
1964 May 30	**Little Eastern**	R G Wilson E Townsend
1964 August 15	**The Arrow**	H I Banner R G Wilson
1965 April 3	**The Key**	J Brown D E Alcock
1965 April 30	**The Far East Girdle**	J Brown D E Alcock
1965 June 2	**Sinistra**	J Brown J Cheesmond
1965 July 4	**Aries**	D E Alcock B A Fuller
1965 August 20	**Trapeze**	T Herley D Blythe

1965 October 6	**Diwedd Groove**	R Edwards M A Boysen
	The final section was added by R Edwards and D Mellor on October 10.	
1966 April 30	**Spartacus**	R Edwards A Harris
1966 May 29	**Chicane**	P Crew G Birtles
1966 May 29/30	**Mynedd**	R Edwards R Evans M Eldrich
1966 May 30	**Thrombin**	P Crew Miss J Baldock
1966 August 22	**Fibrin**	R Edwards J Costello
1966 October 14	**New Girdle, West Buttress**	R Edwards E G Penman
1968 June 14	**Route 68**	D S Potts B Ingle *(Alternate leads)*
1969	**Mordor**	C Phillips R Kirkwood
1970 May 23	**Apollo**	L Dickinson B Molyneaux
1970 June	**Gemini**	A Rouse L Dickinson
1970 July	**Flintstone Wall**	G J Gilbert A S Cole
1970	**Easy Rider**	D Yates D S Potts
1971 May 22	**Syth**	D E Alcock M A Boysen A Hunt D Jones
	Pitches 4 and 5 were added by D E Alcock and A Hunt on May 26.	
1971 June 4	**Gormod**	D Alcock A Hunt *(Varied leads)*
1971 July 17	**The Leech**	R Evans J Pasquill *(Alternate leads)*
	The Direct Finish was climbed by A Rouse and R Carrington in 1975.	
1971 July 17	**Syncope**	R Edwards K Toms

1971 August	**Curving Arête**	R Evans C Rogers
1971 August 17	**Soledad Brother**	D J S Cook B Griffiths
1971 August 22	**Land of Hope and Glory**	L E Holliwell B Whybrow
	The flake crack of pitch 3 was climbed later in 1971 by L E Holliwell, J W Kingston and R Ford.	
1971 August 22	**Stomach Traverse**	R Evans C Rogers
1971 September 17	**Jelly Roll**	R Evans C Rogers
1972 July 25	**Sea of Cloud**	G Milburn D Gregory *(Alternate leads)*
1972 July 27	**Sun Dance**	G Milburn D Gregory *(Alternate leads)*
1972 August 23	**The Republican**	D J S Cook J Perrin *(Alternate leads)*
1972 August 29	**Road of Ghosts**	G Milburn C Griffiths *(Alternate leads)*
1973 July 7	**Prominus**	J Tout A Strapcans
1973 August	**Capricorn**	R Newcombe J Whittle
	Climbed free on the second ascent by A Sharp and C Dale on June 23 1975.	
1973 August 25	**Wapentake**	G Milburn D Gregory *(Varied leads)*
1973 August 25	**Adam's Rib**	D Gregory G Milburn *(Alternate leads)*
1973 August 26	**White Rose Garland**	G Milburn D Gregory *(Alternate leads)*
1974	**Metamorphosis**	C Phillips M Barnicott
1974 March 30	**Illegal Eagle**	A Strapcans M Barnicott
1974 June 29	**Quiver**	P Bartlett A Brazier

1975 May 17	**Rumplestiltskin**	A Strapcans C King
1975 May 23	**Silhouette**	R Edwards N Metcalfe
1975 June 8	**The Spire**	A Strapcans C King
1975 June 11	**Blancmange Sandwich**	A Sharp S Humphries
1975 June 22	**Beano**	C Phillips M Crook
1975 June 29	**Head for Heights**	C Phillips N J Escourt
1975 July 4	**The Sweeper**	R Edwards N Metcalfe
1975 August 29	**Medi**	R Edwards T Jepson

Numerical Pitch Gradings

The following list is of routes of Very Severe and above in the order in which they appear in the guide. The figures in brackets after the adjectival grades indicate the number of any points of aid used. Six routes have been omitted from this list due to lack of information.

Boomerang	5a,5a	HVS
Soledad Brother	5a,5b	HVS
Little Eastern	4c,3b	VS
Brwynog Chimney	3b,4c	VS
The Key	3b,5a,-	MXS(1)
Sinistra	5b,5a,5a,-	XS(1)
Woubits Left Hand	5b,5b,6a	XS
Woubits	5b,5b,-	XS
The Mostest	4a,5a,5b,3a	MXS
Naddyn Ddu	4a,4b,(5c),5c,4a	XS(2)
Far East Girdle	3b,5a,-,5a,5a,-	MXS(2)
The Sceptre	5b,3a	HVS
The Orb	4b,4c,3a	VS
Slurp	5a	HVS
The Republican	5a,4c,4c,4a	HVS
Rumplestiltskin	5b	MXS
Mostest Direct Start	5c,-	XS
Chicane	5a,-	MXS(2)
Stomach Traverse	4c,5a,4c	XS(3)
Route 68	4c,4c,-	VS
Land of Hope and Glory	-,4b,5b,4c	XS(1)
Gormod	4b,5b,5b	MXS(4)
Little Krapper	5b,-	HVS
Beanlands	5a,-,4c	HVS
East Gully Wall	5c(5c),4c,4c(4c,5a)	MXS
Shrike	5c,5a	MXS
East Gully Groove	4c(5b),3b	VS
The Croak	4c,5b,5a,4b	MXS
Gargoyle	3b(5b),5a,-,4b	HVS
Aries	3b,4c,4b	VS
Octo	4a,5a	HVS
The Hand Traverse	5c,4a	XS
Pinnacle Arête	5b,-	MXS
Taurus	5b	XS
Spillikin	4c,4a	HVS
Guinevere	5b,4c	HVS

Pinnacle Flake	5b,4b	MXS
The Spire	5b,5b	MXS
The Pinnacle Girdle	5b,5b,5b,5c,5b,-,5a,-,5a	XS
Sunset Crack	-,3a,4a,4c,-,	VS
Serth	5b,5b,-	XS
The Leech	5a,5c,5c(5c)	XS
Llithrig	3a,5a,4c,4c,-	HVS(1)
Capricorn	4a,5a,5a,5c	MXS
Pigott's Climb	4a,4b,3b,5a	VS
Wall Variations	5b,5a,4c,4a	MXS
Trapeze	5a,-,5c,-	XS(3)
The Sweeper	-,5b,-	MXS
Chimney Route	3b,4a,3a,4c(4c)(4c),4a	VS
Diglyph	3b,5b,4c	HVS
Daurigol	5b,5c,4c	XS
Great Wall	6a,6a	HXS
The Arête Finish	5b	MXS
Blancmange Sandwich	5c	XS
Jelly Roll	5a,5b,5b	XS
November	5a,5c,5a	XS
Vember	5a,5b,4a	MXS
Medi	5c	XS(1)
Curving Crack	4c,4b,4c	VS
Curving Arête	4c,5b	HXS
Troach	4c,5b,5a	XS
Pedestal Crack	5a,4c,4b	VS
Scorpio	5b	XS
Silhouette	5c,5c	XS
The Corner	5a	HVS
The Shadow	4c,5c,4c	XS
Mordor	5c	XS(3)
Terrace Crack	3b,4a,4c	VS
East Buttress Girdle	3a,5a,4c,4c,4a,5a,-,4a,-,-,5a	HVS(1)
Moonshine	-,5a,-(5a)	HVS
Birthday Crack	4a,4c	VS
Prominus	4c,-	VS
Adam's Rib	4b,3b,4a	VS
Flintstone Wall	5a,5a,	HVS
Illegal Eagle	5a,-	HVS
Left Edge	4a,4c,3b	HVS
The Boulder	4a,5a,5a(4b),-	HVS
Gemini	5b,5c	XS
The Boldest	5b,(5b)	XS
The Black Cleft	3b,5b,5b,5a,-	MXS
Longland's Climb	4a,4b,3b,4c(4b)(5a)	VS

Ghecko Groove	5a,5b(5c)	XS
White Slab	5a,4b,5a,-(5c),5a,3b,4c	MXS(1)
West Buttress Eliminate	5b,5c,5b,5b	XS
Sheaf	4c,4c,3b,3a,4a,4c,4c,-	VS
Sheaf Direct	5c,-,5b,5a	XS
Narrow Slab	4c,4c,3a,4c,4c,4a,-	VS
The Arrow	5b,-	XS(1)
Quiver	5b	XS
Bow-Shaped Slab	4c,4a,3a,3b,4c,4b,-	VS
Bow Right Hand	5a,5c,4c	XS
Great Slab	4c,4a,(-,4c),4b,3a,3b	VS
Syth	5c,5a,-,5b,-	XS(1)
Moss Groove	-,4c,-	HVS
Central Rib	4b,4c,-,-	VS
Mynedd	-,5b,5b,5a,-	XS(1)
Spartacus	-,5b,-	MXS & A3
Slanting Slab	5a,4a,5a	MXS(3)
Gael	5b,5a,5a	XS(3)
Fibrin	5a,5a,-	MXS(4)
Thrombin	5a,-	MXS
Bloody Slab	5b(5a),5a,-	XS
Syncope	5b,5b,-	XS(2)
Haemogoblin	5b,5b,-	MXS
Carpet Slab	4c,4a	VS
Diwedd Groove	4c,5c,-	XS(2)
West Buttress Girdle	-,4c,3b,3a,4a,4c,4c,4c,4c,5a, 4b,4c,-,-,-,-,-	HVS
New Girdle	-,5a,5a,-,-,5c,5a,4c,4c,4c,5a, -,5b,5a,5a,5a,5b,-,-,-	XS(6)
Beano	5c	XS(1)
Steep Band	4c,5a	VS
Head for Heights	-,5c	XS(4)
Wapentake	3a,4a,4b,3a,-	VS
Sea of Cloud	4b,4c,3b	VS
Road of Ghosts	4c,4c,-	VS
Sun Dance	4a,4b,4a,-	VS

Index of Climbs

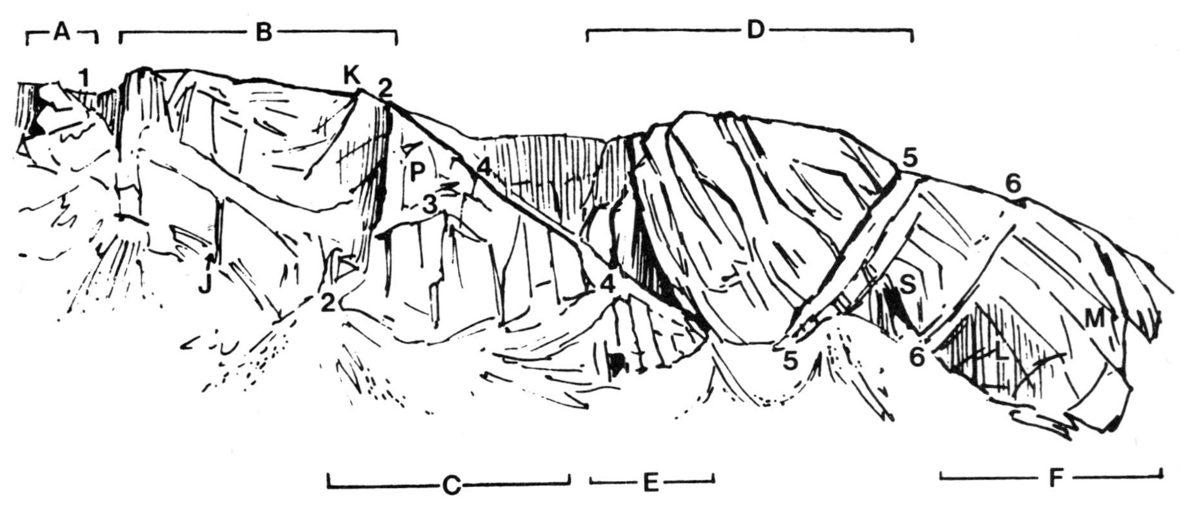
A
B
D
1
K
2
P
3
4
5
6
J
2
4
S
M
L
5
6
C
E
F

The Main Features of the Cliff

Key		Page
A	The Far Far East Buttress	9
B	The Far East Buttress	10
C	The East Buttress	24
D	The West Buttress	35
E	The Middle Rock	34
F	The Far West Buttress	54
P	The Pinnacle	18
S	The Steep Band	52
1	The Far Eastern Terrace	10

	Page	Key
East Gully	17	**2**
Green Gallery	24	**3**
The Eastern Terrace	24	**4**
The Western Terrace	35	**5**
The Far Western Terrace	54	**6**
Jubilee Climb	15	**J**
Camus	17	**K**
Slanting Chimney	54	**L**
Deep Chimney	57	**M**

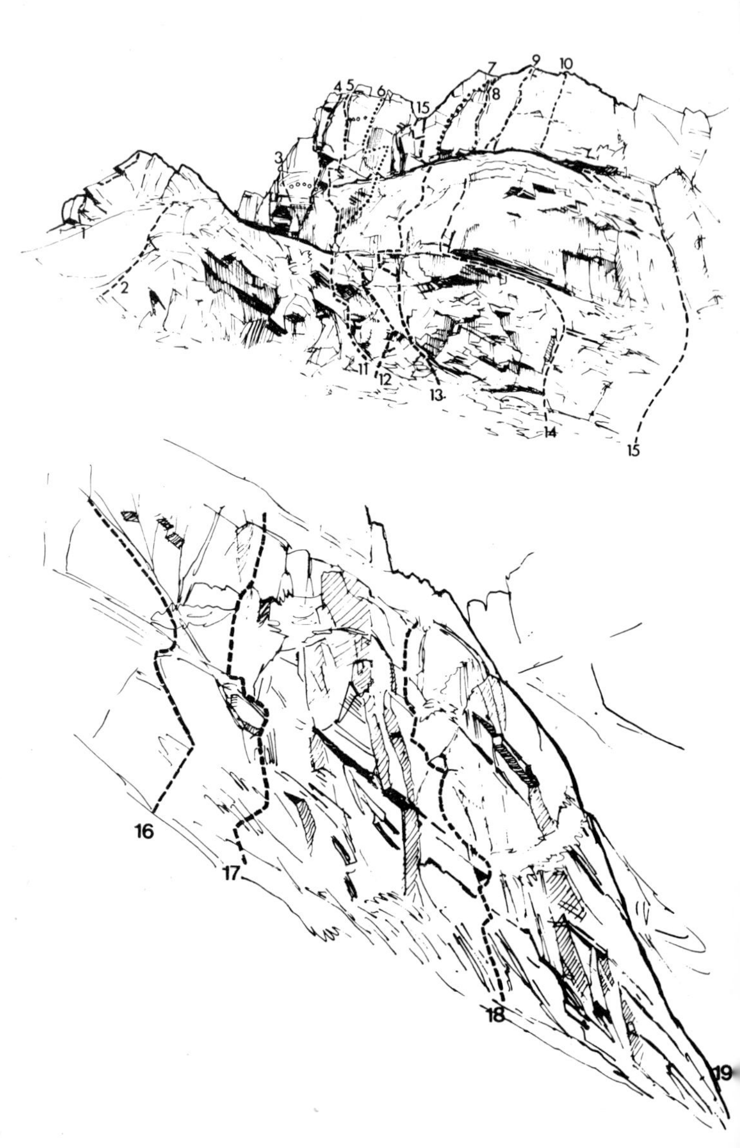
1
2
3
4 5
6
15
7
8
9
10
11
12
13
14
15
16
17
18
19

The Far Far East and Far East Buttresses

Key		Grade	Page
1	Boomerang	HVS	9
2	Little Eastern	VS	9
3	Sinistra	XS	10
4	Woubits	XS	11
5	The Mostest	MXS	11
6	Naddyn Ddu	XS	12
7	The Sceptre	HVS	13
8	The Orb	VS	13
9	The Bauble	VS	13
10	Slurp	HVS	13
11	Rumplestiltskin	MXS	14
12	Mostest Direct Start	XS	14
13	Chicane	MXS	14
14	Stomach Traverse	XS	14
15	Jubilee Climb	S	15
16	Route 68	VS	15
17	Land of Hope and Glory	XS	16
18	Gormod	MXS	16
19	Little Krapper	HVS	16

6
7
4
5
2
3
1
7
2
3
1
7
4
6

The Far East Buttress — Woubits Area

Key		Grade	Page
1	Brwynog Chimney	VS	10
2	The Key	MXS	10
3	Sinistra	XS	10
4	Woubits	XS	11
5	Woubits Left Hand	XS	11
6	The Mostest	MXS	11
7	Naddyn Ddu	XS	12
ooo	The Girdle Traverse	MXS	12

1
2
3a
3
3b
4
5
6
7
8
9
10
11
12

The Pinnacle — East Gully Wall Face

Key		Grade	Page
1	East Gully	VD	17
2	Beanlands	HVS	18
3	East Gully Wall	MXS	18
3a	Direct Start	XS	18
3b	Moseley's Variation	HVS	19
4	Shrike	MXS	19
5	East Gully Groove	VS	19
6	The Croak	MXS	19
7	Easy Rider	VS	20
8	Gargoyle	HVS	20
9	Aries	VS	20
10	The Hand Traverse	XS	21
11	Octo	HVS	21
12	Pinnacle Arête	MXS	21
ooo	Pinnacle Girdle	XS	23

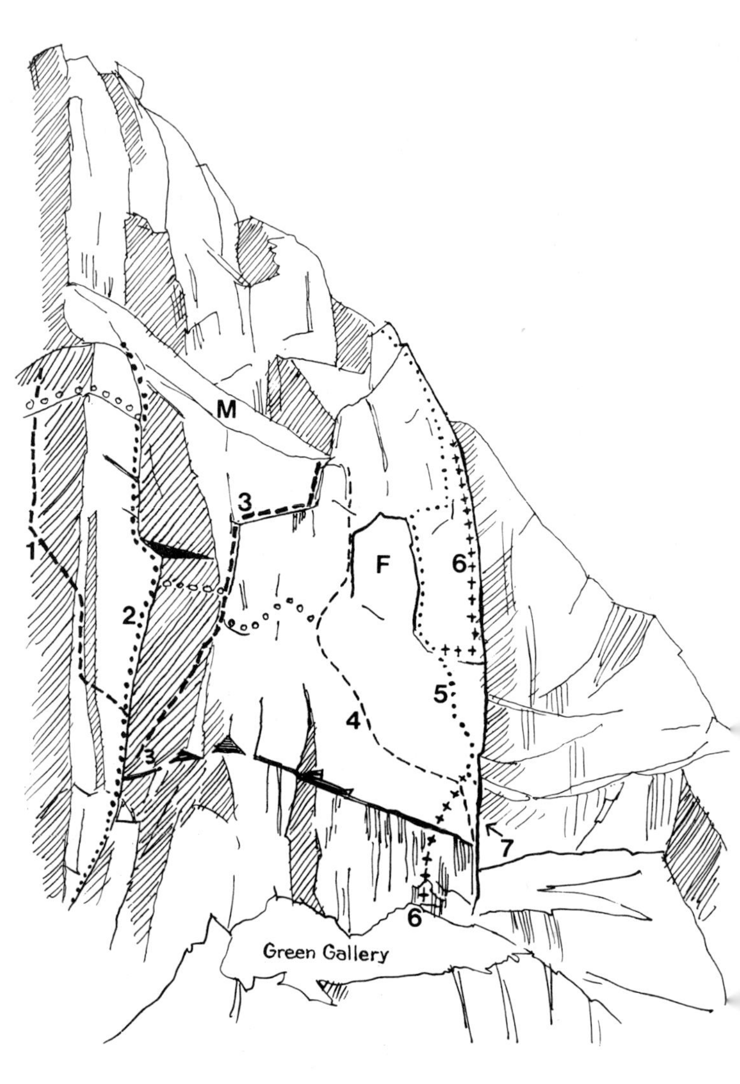
M
3
F
1
2
6
5
4
3
7
6
Green Gallery

The Pinnacle Face

Key		Grade	Page
1	Pinnacle Arête	MXS	21
2	Taurus	XS	21
3	Spillikin	HVS	22
4	Guinivere	HVS	22
5	Pinnacle Flake	MXS	22
6	The Spire	MXS	22
7	Direct Finish to the East Buttress	HS	22
M	The Meadow		22
F	The Flake		22

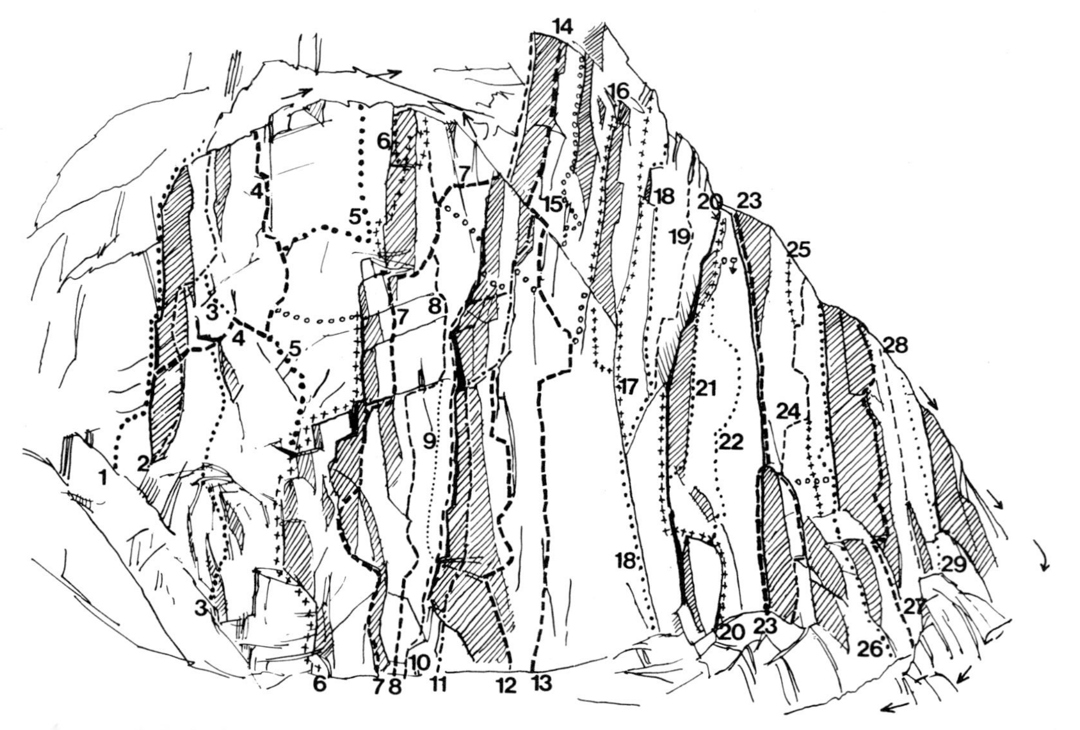
14
16
6
4
7
15
18
20
23
5
19
25
3
8
4
7
5
28
17
21
24
9
22
2
1
18
29
3
27
20
23
26
10
6
7 8
11
12
13

The East Buttress

Key		Grade	Page
1	Sunset Crack	VS	24
2	Serth	XS	25
3	The Leech	XS	25
4	Llithrig	HVS	26
5	Capricorn	MXS	26
6	Pigott's Climb	VS	26
7	Wall Variations	MXS	27
8	Trapeze	XS	27
9	The Sweeper	MXS	27
10	Chimney Route	VS	28
11	Diglyph	HVS	28
12	Daurigol	XS	28
13	Great Wall	HXS	29
14	The Arête Finish	MXS	29
15	Blancmange Sandwich	XS	29

	Grade	Page	Key
Jelly Roll	XS	29	16
November	XS	30	17
Vember	MXS	30	18
Medi	XS	30	19
Curving Crack	VS	30	20
Curving Arête	HXS	31	21
Troach	XS	31	22
Pedestal Crack	VS	31	23
Scorpio	XS	31	24
Silhouette	XS	32	25
The Corner	HVS	32	26
The Shadow	XS	32	27
Mordor	XS	32	28
Terrace Crack	VS	32	29
The East Buttress Girdle	HVS	33	ooo

13
11
7
15
6
10
9
12
a
3
4
5
western terrace
15
6
7
14
a
1
2

The Middle Rock, the West Buttress and the Steep Band

Key		Grade	Page
1	Moonshine	HVS	34
2	Birthday Crack	VS	34
3	Left Edge	HVS	37
4	The Boulder	HVS	37
5	The Black Cleft	MXS	38
6	Narrow Slab	VS	41
7	Great Slab	VS	43
8	Slanting Slab	MXS	46

	Grade	Page	Key
Gael	XS	46	9
Bloody Slab	XS	47	10
Haemogoblin	MXS	48	11
Carpet Slab	VS	48	12
Diwedd Groove	XS	48	13
Steep Band	VS	52	14
Mynedd	XS	45	15
easy descent path		35	a

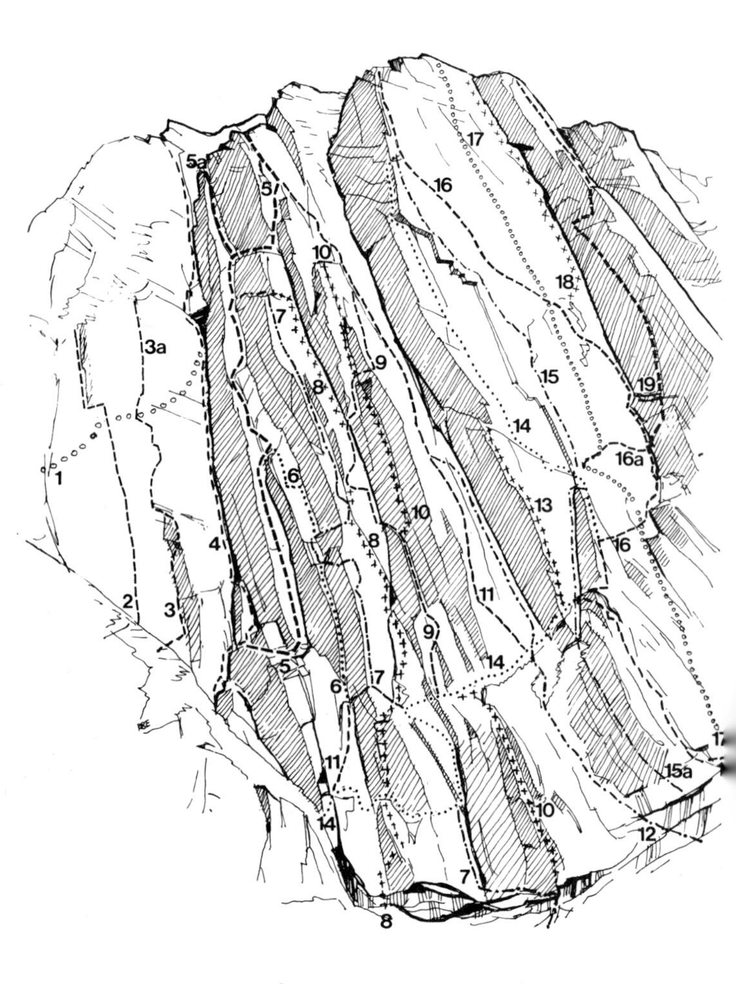

17
16
5a
5
10
18
7
3a
9
8
15
19
14
16a
1
6
13
10
8
16
4
11
2
3
9
14
5
7
6
11
15a
10
14
12
7
8

The West Buttress — Left hand section

Key		Grade	Page
1	The Boulder	HVS	37
2	Gemini	XS	37
3	The Boldest	XS	38
3a	Direct Finish	XS	38
4	The Black Cleft	MXS	38
5	Longland's Climb	VS	38
5a	The Direct Finish	HVS	39
6	Ghecko Groove	XS	39
7	White Slab	MXS	39
8	West Buttress Eliminate	XS	40
9	Sheaf	VS	41
10	Sheaf Direct	XS	41
11	Narrow Slab	VS	41
12	The Arrow	XS	42
13	Quiver	XS	42
14	Bow-Shaped Slab	VS	42
15	Bow Right Hand	XS	43
15a	Direct Start	VS	43
16	Great Slab	VS	43
16a	The Top Traverse	VS	44
17	Syth	XS	44
18	Moss Groove	HVS	44
19	Central Rib	VS	45

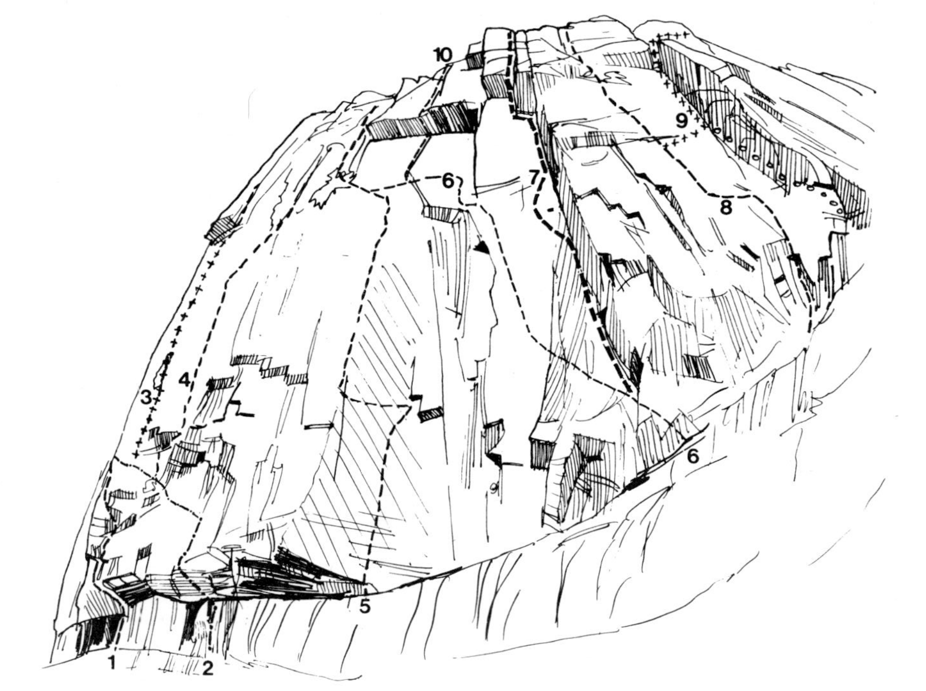

10
9
6
7
8
4
3
6
5
1
2

The West Buttress-Right hand section

Key		Grade	Page
1	Spartacus	MXS/A3	46
2	Slanting Slab	MXS	46
3	Gael	XS	46
4	Fibrin	MXS	46
5	Thrombin	MXS	47

	Grade	Page	Key
Bloody Slab	XS	47	6
Haemogoblin	MXS	48	7
Carpet Slab	VS	48	8
Diwedd Groove	XS	48	9
Syncope	XS	47	10

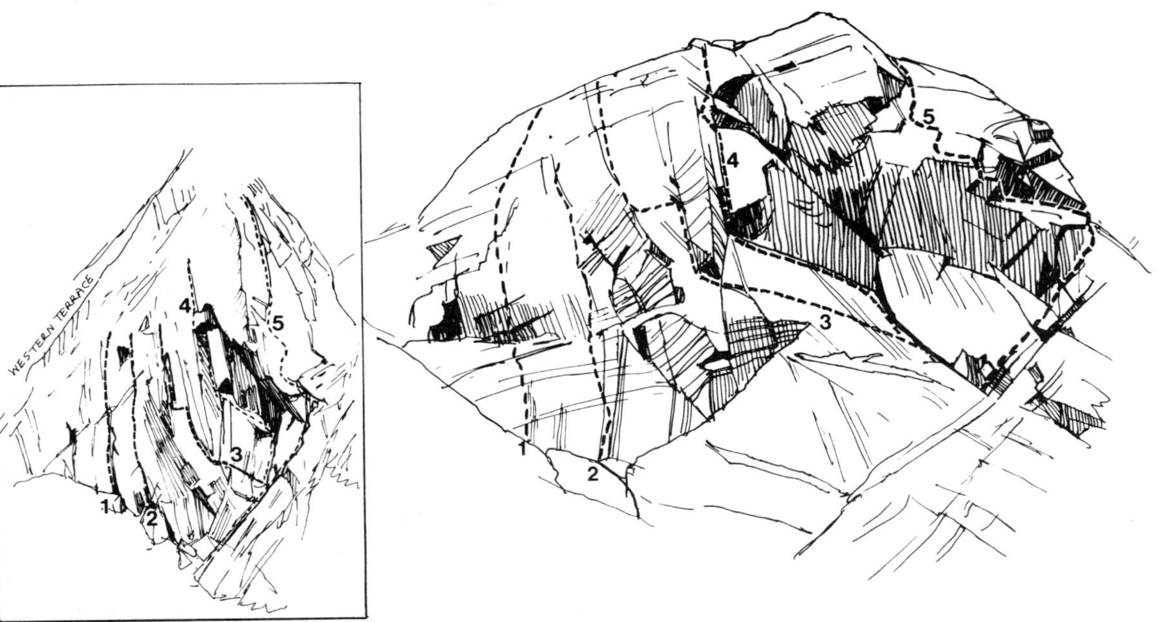

WESTERN TERRACE
4
5
3
1
2
5
4
3
1
2

The Steep Band (Distant and Close-up)

Key		Grade	Page
1	Metamorphosis	VS	52
2	Beano	XS	52
3	Steep Band	VS	52

	Grade	Page	Key
Apollo	MXS/A1	52	**4**
Head for Heights	XS	53	**5**

Mountain Rescue

Persons suffering from minor injuries can be evacuated from the cliff by improvised methods, but caution must prevail as minor injuries can be aggravated by rough treatment.

In the event of an accident where assistance is required, a message giving all the factual information about the person(s), location (climb, pitch etc.) should be passed on to the North Wales Police at the Police Station Llanberis (Telephone Llanberis 222), or at the Headquarters (Telephone Colwyn Bay 57171), or by dialling 999. During the season, assistance can be summoned via the Snowdon Mountain Railway at the Clogwyn and Halfway satations. The informant should remain by the telephone in case further information is required.

The Police will contact the respective Rescue Team/Post, and as co-ordinators will obtain further assistance and request the assistance of a helicopter as directed by those effecting the rescue. All normal evacuations will be made from Hafoty Newydd.

After an accident, please report in writing directly to the Hon. Secretary, Mountain Rescue Committee, 9 Milldale Avenue, Temple Meads, Buxton, Derbyshire, giving particulars of: date of accident, extent of injuries, name, age and address of the casualty, details of the MRC equipment used and the amount of morphia used (so that it can be replaced). Normally this will be done by the local Police and/or the Rescue Post/Team involved, who will also require the names and addresses of the persons climbing with the injured party.

Avoid making rash or unconsidered statements to the press; refer any journalists to the mountaineer who has overall charge of the rescue.

HELICOPTER NOTES

In the event of a helicopter evacuation ALL climbers ON or OFF the cliff should take heed. A helicopter flying close to the cliff will make verbal communications between climbers difficult, and small stones etc will be dislodged by the rotor downdraft. All loose equipment must be secured and climbers in precarious positions should try to make themselves safe. A smoke grenade may be dropped from the helicopter to give the wind direction.

The persons with the injured party should try to identify their location. NO attempt should be made to throw a rope at the helicopter, but assistance should be given to the helicopter crew/rescue personnel if requested.

A helicopter will always be flown into the wind to effect a rescue and on landing there are three danger points: the main rotor, the tail rotor and the engine exhaust. The helicopter should not be approached until directed to do so by the air crew.

New Climbs

NEW CLIMBS

NEW CLIMBS

NEW CLIMBS

NEW CLIMBS

NEW CLIMBS